The Nation Will Follow

Firsthand Experiences Fighting the Deep State and the Action Plan for the American Citizen

#GOTCC Get Off the Couch and Get in the Game

Pierucci Publishing books may be purchased in bulk at special discounts for sales promotion, corporate gifts, fund-raising or educational purposes. Special editions can be created to specifications. For details, contact the Sales Department, Pierucci Publishing, PO Box 8067, Aspen, CO 81612 or publishing@pieruccipublishing.com.

Visit our website at www.pieruccipublishing.com

Paperback ISBN: 978-1-956257-57-1
Hardcover ISBN: 978-1-956257-54-0
Ebook ISBN: 978-1-956257-55-7

Cover Design by Stephanie Pierucci
Edited by Dale Chaplin
Formatting by Sophie Hanks

Proudly printed in the United States of America.

DISCLAIMER

Names, characters, business, events, and incidents have been modified for the purposes of conveying a narrative. Any resemblance to actual persons, living or dead, or actual events is purely coincidental

DEDICATION

To the American citizen who yearns for a constitutional America and a US government owned and directed by the American people. This is the vision that many around the world seek in their own country or choose to come to America so they can live this aspiration.

Preface

By Stephen K. Bannon

The MAGA Whitaker Chambers

Colonel John Mills spent his life as a warrior dedicated to the 'defense of the realm', from the centers of power in the Pentagon to foreign battlefields. The book you have in your hand 'The Nation Will Follow' tells the story of his journey from unquestioning foot soldier to fire-breathing America First Patriot. His 'Damascene Moment' on this journey— in the A-ring of the Pentagon itself when in the run-up to the 2016 Presidential election a long-trusted colleague whispers 'We see more opportunities with Her'.

This book is a full-on assault at The Administrative State's most rogue and dangerous element— the Deep State component of the National Security and Intelligence apparatus that has now been turned on the American People as a form of oppression and control. Colonel Mills comes forth in this book as he did in real life — to be a witness for truth and to talk that truth to power. As a whistleblower to the Durham investigation, you will watch him go up against that power and get a first-hand look at the possibilities I believe Durham and Barr squandered.

Whitaker Chambers is renowned in American history as an atheist and communist who converted to Christianity and publicly denounced the elitist paragon of the Administrative State Alger Hiss. This happened right after the Second World War at the very moment America squandered her victory because of communist infiltration into the highest levels of our government. Whitaker gave witness to Hiss's betrayal, his lies, his treason.

And so now does Colonel John Mills.

'The National Will Follow' does not stop there— Mills offers a clarion call to the populist nationalist movement—a call that is very simple yet very hard— 'no one is coming to save you'. The salvation of this Republic, the possibility of handing down to future generations the Nation that was bequeathed to us is all dependent upon human agency. Your agency.

John Mills is cut from the mold of the classic American hero of 'Shane' … not looking for a fight, but when pushed to the limit will stand and fight for liberty, justice, and freedom.

Strategic Context

By the Honorable Ty McCoy

The "Nation Will Follow" by Colonel (Ret.) John Mills is a vital message to the citizens of the United States and should be read and remembered every day. The book lays out the nature of the corruption in our society, provides specific examples from John's experience, and provides a plan of action to preserve our hard-won, but disappearing, freedoms and prosperity and security.

I have known John for several years and watched as he has tried to understand and root out corruption in the Pentagon, other government entities, and discover and expose election corruption. His energy, experience, dedication in pursuing the massive corruption of the Deep State in concert with corrupt, mortal adversaries is authentic and compelling. He has witnessed corrupt officials in action and dissected how they have undertaken plots to thwart the will of the voters by undercutting honestly elected officials and by preventing honest elections from occurring.

His message is that there is a well-funded, highly educated, and relentless group of corrupt, elite, powerful people seeking to maintain control of the American government, economy, academia, the media, big tech, unions, religious groups, and now even the military and intelligence services for their own personal benefit and that of their corrupt families and friends. The American people have been their enemy for years, but now the corrupt

Deep State mafia (in government and outside) actively call out the American people as lowlifes, racists, whiners, scumbags, ignorant fools, religious bigots, anti-immigrants, antisocial, antihuman, anti-climate, anti-environment, haters, liars, cheats, and much more, when in fact, they themselves are the very words they use to describe their enemy—the American people. That is why these words come so easy to them. Their defense of their own corrupt souls is to stay on the offense against the American people and use the very characteristics of their twisted souls to broadcast their false and evil disinformation through every legal, illegal, and unseen channel that they can conceive. Telling the Big Lie told in a steady Big Way is what they hope will allow their small but powerful anti-American group to continue its control of our families, wealth, values, and freedoms.

The prescription by the author to learn and earn your way into county (city and state) government is a good plan of action. Whoever controls the counties will control elections and thus state and federal government (and local education and law enforcement and property rights, etc.). Colonel Mills's methods have worked, and he has put them to the test.

Indeed, without religious piety to govern human relations, the rule of law to constrain political relations, and capitalism to manage economic matters, the corrupt factions will continue to run rampant.

Having seen the same growing corruption in the US government and society, as an insider and outsider at the highest levels, I urge you to read, understand, discuss, organize, and act before your rights to do so are taken from you—and not to be returned to you and your families. Do it for your parents, yourselves, your kids, and for free people everywhere.

V/R

Honorable Tidal W. McCoy, Acting Secretary, Department of the Air Force, (Retired)

Table of Contents

Prologue 13

PART ONE

Chapter One : Moms Are the Tip of the Spear 19

Loudoun County 21

Byde My Time? 23

They Are Society's Children - Not Yours...27

Chapter Two : Encounter on the "A" Ring 31

"We See More Opportunities With Her"..32

Who Is We and What Opportunities Do You See?....................................35

Chapter Three : What is the Deep State? 37

Cult of the Swamp Narrative..40

What Is It? 43

Who Is It?..47

PART TWO

Chapter Four : I Know They Exist, Here's How **55**

The Original Deplorable 57

Dinner in London 60

Palace Intrigue 66

Chapter Five : Stop Trump **71**

Comey, Brennan, and ICA Lies 74

Finding Top Cover 76

Who Can You Trust? A Four-Year Pathway to Durham 81

Chapter Six : A Life of Service **87**

My Witness 90

God, Family, Country 92

Breaching the Berm 96

Psyops in Bosnia 101

Chapter Seven : The Day the World Changed **109**

Return to Your Home Station 111

America United 114

America Divided 116

PART THREE

Chapter Eight : The Four Corners of Deceit **121**

Big Government 123

Big Academia 126

Big Tech 128

Big Finance 130

All of Which Leads to Globalism 131

Chapter Nine : How Societies Collapse **135**

They Become Wealthy and Affluent 137

They Lose Their Foundation 139

They Lose Their Drive 141

Chapter Ten : A Return to Election Integrity............................145

Give Me the Mic!...147

Seize Your Mic Opportunity 148

Local Civilian/Citizen/Patriot POWER: The Loudoun County Effect   150

There Is No One Else, There Is Only Us.................................153

Chapter Eleven : Taking Back Control.....................................157

The Beginnings of the Deep State Takeover 158

The County Is the Center of Gravity.....................................164

Get Off the Couch and Get in the Game 166

Chapter Twelve : The Portrait of a Great America 169

Citizens Are Actively Leading Their Counties 170

Secure Your County and the Nation Will Follow 172

A Constitutional, America First Model Starting with the County   175

Bonus 182

Prologue

A witness, in the sense that I am using the word, is a man whose life and faith are so completely one that when the challenge comes to step out and testify for his faith, he does so, disregarding all risks, accepting all consequences.

Whittaker Chambers

This book is an action briefing. In the military, there are often two types of briefing: the action briefing and the information briefing. An information briefing provides you with information. It tells you the lay of the land, the state of play, what is happening, and why it is happening.

An information briefing has its uses. With an information briefing, we can assess our views of a given situation, address our preconceptions, and begin to make plans as to how we move forward.

The inherent problem with an information briefing is that it leaves all the planning and implementation to us. It falls short of providing a tangible plan or set of goals with which we can move forward. It simply tells us what is, not what we should do. Without this crucial part, and without a unified direction of travel underpinned by credible and concrete leaders, action is aimless and ineffective.

Sure, it may occasionally lead to some pretty spectacular bangs, but bangs are just that. They are flashes in the pan. They are short-lived. Without momentum, they evaporate, disappear, and are quickly forgotten about.

Many authors, news outlets, and key thinkers in this daily information battle for America live squarely within this realm of providing information briefings. They have performed admirable work in bringing to light the daily crimes, cover-ups, and acts of treason that are committed by the Deep State that exists to subvert and undermine our great democracy. I commend them for this.

It is because of the work of these brave people that there is now a widespread acceptance of the Deep State[1] in mainstream America. A recent Rasmussen Number of the Day (August 9, 2022) showed that only 16 percent say there is definitely "No Deep State" and 64 percent feel there "Is a Deep State." Despite a stiff-necked campaign to ignore, mock, or plain lie, a growing number—now in the plurality—know something was greatly amiss in November 2020.

I was asked at a recent federal hearing about my view on this matter. I said words to the effect that Joe Biden is the sworn president, and at the same time, I have grave concerns over what happened in November 2020. These two views are not mutually exclusive. Both can be true at the same time.

However, what is missing is a plan of action, a guide as to what happens next. There is no true blueprint or set of actions that we, as concerned citizens, can adopt and follow to take back control and proceed in a unified way, all singing to the same hymn sheet.

---

1. I will predominantly use the term Deep State. Other relevant terms are the Fourth Branch of Government, Administrative State, Globalists, Nanny Staters, Elite, etc. This is not simplistic name-calling. There is a clear movement of people and groups that seeks to subjugate citizens in America and around the world because they know better and the citizen is stupid. I have heard various examples of this expression and feeling before in meetings in the Eisenhower Executive Office Building (EEOB) next to the White House. Simply put, there are those who feel that citizens are too stupid to understand the brilliant things that are being done for them.

My goal is to fix that. Through this book, I aim to provide you, a soldier in our new war for independence, with an action briefing, a series of guides and instructions as to what we can do next.

To do this, I have used a combination of what I know from my time working in the upper echelons of the US government and the US military, and the examples given to us by the pioneering few who have set the bar and the example for us all to follow.

In writing this book, my team and I have spoken to many loyal, brave, and pioneering individuals who are leading the fight and the charge against the Deep State.

They are not doing it with guns and violence, they are using the very tools that the Deep State is looking to suppress, their voices and the tools of democracy. Citizens are standing their ground where they live. They are doing their best to secure their county to secure America.

Their stories are inspiring, and throughout this book, I will draw upon these and provide reference to their immense collective wisdom, and you will see as you progress through this book that these "soldiers" are not soldiers in the conventional sense; they are your average men, women, moms, dads, and standard, run-of-the-mill citizens.

Only, they are not. They are brave pioneers, voyagers that have taken the first confident and bold steps in the fight against the Deep State. These ordinary people are just like you and me.

They come from across the political spectrum, spanning multiple races, ethnicities, occupations, political affiliations, and, most poignantly, genders. One thing is certain, it is not up to any one group or demographic. We all have the ability to fight the Deep State. We all have the right, and we all have the need.

Our first struggle as a nation against tyranny came in the fight for our independence. We think of this war as a popular uprising, of everyone picking up guns and swords and taking the fight to the British. This is categorically not how it happened.

The American Revolution was fought by roughly 3 percent of the population. You did not misread that. *Three percent.* Three percent mobilized, took up arms, and fought the British. This 3 percent was supported by a further 10 percent: loved ones, friends and family, and like-minded people. Much of the 10 percent consisted of pastors leading their flocks.

This means that our nation-defining struggle was actively fought for by only 13 percent of the people. But when that 13 percent won, that other 87 percent came along for the ride, switched allegiances, and backed the winning horse. The fence-sitting phenom is not new or unique. I have been in several conflicts, low- and high-end, and fence-sitting is the norm for imperfect humans trying to survive in the chaos. But no matter what you think, how insurmountable the opposition may seem, the battle can be won by a slim few. The rest will join as the momentum builds.

For those of us who are aware and have the knowledge but are unsure of what to do next, this is for you.

For those of us who are sitting on the fence unsure of what to believe, what to think, and who to listen to, our political allegiances clouding or falsely informing our judgment, this is for you.

For those of you who have dabbled in the idea of taking action but have fallen short of anything concrete, hesitant, or reluctant to engage, maybe this is the spark you were waiting for. This is for you.

And for those of you who do not believe, justifiably yet falsely reassured by the lies of the mainstream media and politicians, then this book may well ignite your curiosity, convincing you that, maybe, there is something to all of this Deep State stuff. This is for you too.

This book is for everyone because like it or not, you are affected, each and every day, by the Deep State. Together we stand, and together we will fight them.

Part One

Chapter One

Moms Are the Tip of the Spear

"I do honestly think that if women were running the world there would be more investment in peace, because basically as women we do not want to see our children killed. Maybe I am completely idealistic, but until we see women in equal positions of power in the world, I just think that we are doomed."

Meryl Streep

Let me start by explaining that we are at war inside America and worldwide. Unfortunately, war is a normal part of the human continuum. This is not yet a war in the conventional sense, fought with guns and bombs (at least, not on our shores). The war we are fighting and have been for decades is for control and security of right where we live in America—in our counties. The county (or county equivalent for those who use different terms in America), is the foundation of America. Secure your county and the nation will follow.

When the Founding Fathers penned the Constitution and created the government and the structures that would form the Republic, they did so to return power to the people and to cast off the yoke of oppression. The goal was to oppose tyranny, to enact democracy, and to create and protect a society that held the principles of freedom and liberty at its very core. The ambition was simple, the structures rigid, and the public will infallible. The fight for American independence, however, did not end when the British Empire was cast away and the greatest nation on God's Green Earth was born.

This was when it began. In the centuries since, the citizens of America have been engaged in warfare, internal and external, to protect these United States of America. In the American Civil War, liberty was defended through military means, and the Union was solidified.

Since then, the weapon of choice of the high priest of the Deep State has been societal control through incrementalism. They have been relentless in their drive to incrementally and innocuously strip, chip, and contain the citizen. Guns and bombs have given way to control, influence and power, and the war for our freedom and liberty is, to the uninformed, invisible. But when you know how to spot it, suddenly you begin to see it everywhere.

This war has two combatants. The first of these is the Deep State: a seditious group of political and nonpolitical actors using the media, globalism, politics, and mass psychosis to control and sway the citizens of the United States.

On the other side, there is everyone else. I had approximated the split to be 80 percent everyone else and 20 percent in the Deep State camp (the Rasmussen Numbers previously cited were 84/16, so I was low). What I urge all is that we are the majority, so let's start acting like it: the citizens of the US, and therefore, by proxy of the immense global influence of the United States, the citizens of the world. Let me make it clear, the Deep State is not a strictly American phenomenon, it's a global cadre of elitists whose sole purpose is to control and monopolize the world, enacting a form of modern slavery that subverts itself into global consciousness, making it nearly impossible to resist.

But resist it we must, and we need to do it using the same tools that they are using to enact their control and exert their influence. We need to take back control using the tools and the apparatus that our Founding Fathers gave us: our Constitution and our Democracy.

Senator Amanda Chase, who coincidentally is the only legislator in Virginia calling for a full, forensic audit of the election process and stands in solidarity with the Loudoun County moms (being one herself,) told us that "We are fighting darkness and it's time to hold election leaders and elected officials to account." For decades, intrepid patriots have attempted to bring the fight to the Deep State, and for decades, they have failed. The pervasive influence of the Deep Staters and their institutions has been too great to overcome until now.

But one group of people, in particular, have found the right tool, pulled the right lever, and have set the example for how we take the fight to the Deep State and how we do it in a way that means we can win.

Those people are not the people you would typically expect. They are not archetypal, stereotypical, red-blooded American *men*. No, they are women. They are moms, and they are not rural country folk, they are affluent, influential, and angry.

Loudoun County

The history of Loudoun County, Virginia, dates back to the very founding of the first colonies, and it sits at the heart of the history of our Republic, to the extent that, during the War of Independence, it was Loudoun's grain that fed George Washington's Continental Army, giving it the moniker "The Breadbasket of the Revolution." Located in Virginia, Loudoun County sits to the south of the Potomac and is a stone's throw away from the nation's capital, Washington, DC.

A drive around the county will reveal scenic views and historical buildings, coupled with wealthy and affluent towns and the company headquarters of a large number of big tech corporations, including Verizon and Telos. And an immense number of these innocuous, sterile data centers are surrounded by ubiquitous and common security fencing—an indicator of Deep State data storage for the US government.

You see, the thing about Loudoun County is that, in recent years, its population has undergone rapid shifts, especially since the '80s. What once was a primarily agrarian culture has given way to a rise in urbanism brought about by people hailing from and working in DC.

Sure, it still has a burgeoning agrarian foundation—some things do not die easily—but this shift in demographics and culture has seen the median household income in Loudoun County rise to a whopping $147,111, per the census, making it the highest-ranked county in terms of median income that has a population of over sixty-five thousand people.

So, on the face of it, the people of Loudoun County have it all: serene countryside, a strong economy, and considerable wealth. All the perfect ingredients for a quiet and subservient population.

So how is it that this perfect county, with seemingly little to no motivation to challenge the establishment, is at the very center of the battle against the Deep State, against the entrenched institutionalism that threatens the futures of all of us?

There is a reason, you see, that the motto of Loudoun County is *I Byde My Tyme*. Since Lyndon B. Johnson, the county has been staunchly Republican. That is, until Obama in 2008. Since then, all presidential elections have swung in the favor of the Democrats.

That is fine, sometimes population shift means that voting trends sway and shift. That is perfectly normal within the realm of politics. What is troubling, though, is that the county has consistently voted Red in the gubernatorial elections, voting 61 percent in favor of Bob McDonnell just a year after Obama, and replacing two incumbent Democrat delegates a year later.

So how is it that this county that has vehemently opposed Democrat rule since the '60s now voted in favor of Crooked Hillary by 55 percent, and in 2020, voted to elect Sleepy Joe Biden by over 60 percent?

By electoral integrity conducted without strong citizen involvement and oversight, that's how. Painfully obvious and blatant in its implementation. As a result, the citizens of Loudoun County have chosen to bide their time no longer. For many, the time has come.

Byde My Time?

The people leading this charge are not who you would typically think. For a start, they are not men. Yes, there are many men, on both sides of the aisle, who are active combatants against the Deep State. Trump and his closest followers were such men. And women.

There are a group of women in Loudoun County who recognize that the threat posed by the Deep State is a long-term one and it not only impacts them but also future generations. Those future generations begin with their children.

These amazing mothers, who work astoundingly hard to create environments that are safe for their children to grow up in and that grant the highest possible access to opportunities, have awoken to the fact that this opportunity and this safety is being stolen from their children as their hard work is undermined by the traitorous actors that promote the interest of globalists and elites.

And they are angry.

Astoundingly so. Often, I attend rallies and conferences up and down the country. Sometimes, these are virtual. Often, they are face-to-face. Since Biden's "election," many of these have been established to monitor and challenge electoral fraud.

Electoral fraud is a serious issue. Our democracy is underpinned by the fairness of our voting systems. Around the world, there are, and have been, many sham "democracies" in which there appear to be the working principles, apparatus, and infrastructures of a working democracy, but these apparatus and infrastructures are corrupt, broken, exploited by physical force and something far more dangerous: propaganda, lies, and sedition.

One need to look no further than the examples of twentieth century Egypt, where sham "elections" would see National Democratic Party candidates, like Anwar Sadat, win with 97 percent of the popular vote. What was not shown, or publicly broadcast, were the beatings at the polling stations, the vote switching, and the imprisonment of opposition candidates meaning that, in many instances, there was only one candidate on the ballot. Funny, the irony in that party name.

You do not even need to look back that far to see sham democracy in action. Look at Russia and how Putin has created a system in which he is the sole power, a dictator who has been legitimized by a sham democracy of his own making. He rules over Russia with an iron fist, with absolute power, and it is happening right under our noses, blatantly obvious to us all. But we do nothing about it. Even his invasions first of Georgia, and more prominently in Ukraine, have done nothing (to date) to threaten his position as dictator.

Even hypercommunist China and North Korea are "People's Republics." The two most blatantly authoritarian—no, totalitarian—regimes in the world operate sham democracies.

These amazing women from Loudoun County have, however, recognized an even more dangerous truth: you do not need to look overseas to see a sham fake democracy in action. They know that we are living in one and that the threat it poses will hurt their children.

This is not just speculation, that women "seem" to be more politically active in their opposition to the establishment. I have the proof. I have proof in the number of conversations and the phone calls that I receive. The plurality comes from women. From moms.

And this blows a hole wide open in the fake narrative that the national, mainstream, Soros-led media outlets tell you. They lie to you daily, in a pattern that is frighteningly reminiscent of Russia, Egypt, Iraq, Iran, and many of the world's authoritarian "democracies," telling you that women are universally opposed to Trump. That universally, they are progressive/totalitarian, rejecting any notion of conservatism and laughing away the idea of electoral fraud and the Deep State.

I am here to tell you that this is a lie. Women all over America are motivated and inspired to protect our nation and, in doing so, protect their children.

They know that this will not be achieved with guns and bombs. Poignantly and importantly, they do not want this. After all, it is their children who will be the soldiers in any physical conflict. They also know that such situations rarely end well. Just look at the Arab Spring: how many of those nations in which the military took control now operate as functioning democracies? The answer is not many. The military, more often than not, retains an iron grip.

No, they know that the only way we can enact change is through us. Civilians. They are empowered, stronger than ever. Jesus had a sword, and society has given women swords. Now, they want to use them, and I find this amazing. Inspiring.

I remember a time when my mother, like every other woman in the US, was not allowed to take money out of the bank unless her husband was there to provide a spousal signature. It is these archaic, unjust practices that led to women in their droves turning naturally to a system that falsely offered them equality, gave with one hand and took their children with the other.

This has backfired on the Deep State in a big way. Women, rightly, demanded equality, and in receiving it, they have gained the power to challenge the institutions that threaten their futures, especially the Deep State. This power, and their willingness to wield it, is why women will win this war.

I mean nothing against men. I believe that God created men and women separately and uniquely. Each has its strength, and so, there is nothing unbiblical about these women wielding their power.

The Bible is filled with examples of women enacting positive change, doing God's work, and making the world a better place.

Look at Deborah, the only female judge in the history of Christianity. The story of Deborah is an exceptional one and a truly biblical, Christian example of how women can drive powerful change.

Deborah was a priestess and the fourth judge of pre-monarchical Israel, where a judge was the leader of the country. In short, Deborah gathered an army that was ten thousand strong and reunited Israel with the "Promised Land" (modern-day Palestine), which lived under the brutal Canaanite rule, led by King Jabin. Her army attacked and defeated King Jabin's army, led by Sisera, who was coincidentally killed by another woman, Jael.

Deborah then presided over sixty years of peaceful rule, unheard of at the time, and cemented her legacy as one of the great prophets and leaders of the Old Testament.

Deborah is just one example of a powerful, strong woman in the Bible, there are plenty more, but her example shows us that women have the power to be the driving force behind the type of change that society is crying out for as it attempts to throw off the yoke of tyranny propagated by the Deep State.

The world will be saved by western women, and this is biblical. This is goodness. The power the mom has to influence the family runs in direct contravention to the Four Corners of Deceit (which I will explain in greater detail later).

They Are Society's Children - Not Yours

The Deep State wants your children. Let me tell you that now. They do not just want to stuff them in the trunks of their cars and exploit them for their own individual and personal gains, but they want them for their perfect society.

The Deep State wants you to believe that your children are not yours. They want you to believe that your children are "society's children," that they belong to the government, and that they exist only to contribute to their version of society.

That has a very communist ring to it, doesn't it? Everyone belongs to the state and lives to serve the state and its leaders. In these systems, people are tools not individuals. They have no rights. They are easy to manipulate, exploit, and remove if necessary. When I was in the Pentagon, I tried to give everyone that somehow found my telephone number at least fifteen minutes to make their point. My attitude was they owned this government and paid my salary; it was their right to contact me.

I am not just saying this. These words, "society's children," come directly from Klaus Schwab, leader of the World Economic Forum (WEF) and a proud proponent of globalism. There is another joke, the World Economic Forum, a group of elitists who exist to put more money in the coffers of the superrich—the elite—under the guise of generating communal wealth. Globalism does not exist to serve the many, it exists the serve the few, and it does it exceptionally well, convincing us that participation will empower and enrich us all. When I was in the Department of Defense, senior political appointees and careerists would travel to WEF and WEF-like gatherings, and I did not totally understand what was going on. I do now.

So, Santa Klaus wants not to give gifts to your children but to present them instead as gifts to the globalist elites.

And we say no, the parents of Loudoun County say no, alongside millions of other parents across the US. Our children are not tools of the state. They do not belong to the government, to the Deep State.

They are *our* kids. It is for them to determine their own paths, with us as their guides, not the traitors and criminals who profligate and serve the Deep State.

The Four Corners of Deceit (Big Government, Big Tech, Big Finance, and Big Academia) will tell you that "those are not your children, they are society's children." NO. That is insanity. We, as parents, are not going to allow governmental systems to raise our children.

This thesis, this "brave new world" mentality, is one that we reject. We reject it loudly, and we reject it proudly. We do not care what some bureaucrat in the UN wants us to do. We know what we want, and most importantly, we know how to get it.

"Colonel Mills, what do I do? I want to get involved with what's going on in DC!" I hear this often, and always, my answer is the same.

No, control your county, and the country will follow.

I say this because I have been blessed to live a life that has taken me to the halls of the White House, the Capitol Building, and the Pentagon, and I hate to tell you this, but the corruption runs too deep for any of us to be able to go into DC and change things. Look at Trump. He held the highest office, exposed the Deep State, and still, Biden got in. And now we have the shameful and unprecedented act of his residence being raided. They want us to overreact. Don't overreact—secure your county. Don't just show up to vote—volunteer to be a sworn election officer behind the counter and count the vote. With a change in Congress, we're one step closer to squashing the insanity that has set in.

So, we have the tools our Founding Fathers and our democracy gave us. We have to use our democracy to take control of our counties before we build up to Congress and eventually the White House.

This is why I have focused so heavily on Loudoun County. In Loudoun County, a lack of electoral integrity has stolen the county, and therefore control, away from its people, and those people, led by the moms of Loudoun, want it back.

In short, they have demanded a forensic analysis of the 2020 election and have stopped at nothing to ensure that their voices are heard. These moms are passionate, articulate, eloquent, and not afraid of getting their hands dirty at the grassroots level.

In Loudoun, they are motivating their communities, knocking on doors, and speaking in town halls and state Senate meetings. They are getting in front of people and making noise. Amazingly, they are doing this on top of their family and, often, work commitments. And it is shameful that the US Department of Justice and the Federal Bureau of Investigation are flying over and monitoring these gatherings. Shameful, but there will be a day of reckoning for this unlawful behavior and those who are conducting it, including those who did nothing inside the Swamp to question and stop it. Emails and briefings will be released, and it will be revealed who did what and who stood against these activities. As someone says a lot—retain your records for those inside the US government.

They have garnered national attention, you can look them up online, and they are not hard to find. They are leading the shift in the discourse of our questionable elections from the national level to the local because they know that this is how to enact change.

During, and since the election, I have worked closely with many key influential figures in the county, including Pastors Byron Foxx and Michael Edwards. In the words of Pastor Foxx, a figurehead of the Christian community in Virginia: "There's an awakening going on. And it's in Virginia.

It's engagement from the pew. Election integrity. One of the great successes is… vote according to the Bible. We must raise the level of righteousness in Virginia. God hates lawlessness."

The Twelfth Amendment and Article II of our incredible Constitution make it so that the local level is the true center of gravity of the politics of our nation, not the White House as the media would have you believe.

This is where we need to make our stand, not in the corrupted corridors of power.

Chapter Two

Encounter on the "A" Ring

With the Elite controlling society on scale, intellectual consistency and honesty is an impediment. I'll say whatever it takes to control the society isn't too far away from what Stalin was thinking.

Whittaker Chambers

I remember clearly the day that my resolve stiffened and my purpose became crystal clear to me. This brief encounter lives on, burned into my memory by the horror I felt at the sheer audacity of the nature of the encounter and the blatant openness of the corruption.

Throughout that time in my life, when I transitioned into civilian life, I began a career advising policymakers and senior military officials. I was honored, and still am, to be called into service beyond what many of us would conventionally deem to be service. My years in the military were the proudest years of my life, and this pride continued into my civilian career when I continued to serve our nation on the frontline of strategic decision-making. It is hard to explain what I do, but my phone, texts, and various forms of communication are filled with numerous shout-outs for help, requests for my thoughts, and asks for my input on various hard problem sets.

These years, as you'll discover, have been well served, but it was during that time I began to clearly understand the depth and the levels of corruption that exist within the upper echelons of power.

I had, on many occasions, had my hackles raised and my suspicions alerted by various comments and odd nuances of behavior, but one day, one encounter on the "A" Ring of the Pentagon stands apart from all others. It was that day that the true fire was lit inside me, and I was spurred into a course of action that leads me here, now.

"We See More Opportunities With Her"

The Pentagon, the center of military power in the United States and the headquarters of the Department of Defense, is the world's largest office building at a staggering 28.7 acres, or an additional 5.1 acres if you include the inner courtyard. To me, this is representative of the emphasis and the priority that our nation takes on its defense. It dwarfs the White House and is far bigger than Capitol Hill and all the centers of executive, legislative, and judiciary power in the US.

And it needs to be. As the most powerful nation on Earth, with by far the largest and most powerful military and intelligence apparatus in the world, managing and organizing this behemoth requires vast resources and 24/7 attention. After all, the US military is engaged in operations at all times, in every corner of the globe.

As such, my work has often taken me to the Pentagon, and as a result, I have become well acquainted with its layout and its inner workings.

If you did not know, the Pentagon takes the shape of, you guessed it, a pentagon. It has five sides, five floors above ground (and two below), and is organized into five concentric rings, labeled "A" through "E," and five levels above ground, with additional levels below ground.

The "A" Ring is the innermost ring, facing the inner courtyard, with the "E" Ring facing the outside. As these are the only offices with a view of the outside, they are reserved for the highest-ranking officials.

What is truly impressive about the Pentagon is that, despite its massive size, you can get from any two points in the building in under ten minutes—seven if you are in a hurry. And at all times, you are in a hurry.

As a result, there is a lot of intermingling that happens within the building, and there is very little segregation or separation of departments or individuals. This is crucial as the military world moves fast, and people need to be able to reach each other quickly if needed to relay information that requires urgent attention, especially if, in the modern age, people cannot be reached by phone or email because they are in a meeting or such.

This makes the Pentagon a veritable hive of activity, and chance encounters and knocked-over coffees in the corridors are a common occurrence as people rush from area to area or from meetings to meetings. It is not uncommon for people to leave their desks at the last minute, knowing that they could get to their meeting within ten minutes.

This was the case when I had my fateful and unforgettable encounter in the "A" Ring, one that made it painfully clear to me that corruption had oozed its way into the bastion of national security, into the very fortress that keeps us all safe.

It was the summer of 2016, right before the Republican Convention, that fateful one where Trump defied all expectations to be selected to run against Crooked Hillary and would lead to the exposing of the Deep State for the first time by serving members of the Executive—the president no less.

As such, the beehive that is the Pentagon was abuzz with activity and speculation. The constantly evolving food courts and coffee shops were filled with the conversation that typically surrounds such a convention, particularly when we are guaranteed a new commander in chief after eight years of the previous one. Big changes were afoot, which meant big changes in the halls of the Pentagon.

So against this backdrop, and on a hot summer's day, I was rushing along the "A" Ring to a meeting that I was perilously close to running late for. With a stack of papers tucked under my left arm and a coffee in my right hand, I moved with a purpose along the corridor in as close to a run as I could manage without sloshing coffee all down myself. For years I had a boss who was famous across the Pentagon with the speed of her movement, the loudness of her footsteps, and her J. Edgar Hoover reputation for knowing who had done what and not hesitating to remind them of their actions to ensure their support.

In my hurry, I almost walked straight into someone rushing in the opposite direction, and among the awkward side shuffling and muttered apologies, I recognized a familiar face.

This person I recognized had been a Bush (Bush "W") appointee. He was a Republican, through and through, and owed his position to George "W" and the Republican Party. Due to the nature of the time and the polarization of party politics against the backdrop of the 2016 election, the political affiliations of most were fairly well established and well-known.

The reason this face stood out to me, though, was that, as a Bush appointee, seeing him in the building during the time of Obama was odd, and his was not a face I had seen in some time. This raised suspicion in me, particularly due to the proximity of the Republican Convention. My time in the military, and as an advisor and strategist, has honed in me a sixth sense for suspicious activity and BS.

Smiling, I asked, "What are you doing here?"

"I'm providing input into a meeting as a Gray Beard," he said, seemingly eager to carry on, apparently also cutting it close.

"Great!" I said, and to sate my curiosity and suspicion, I adopted a conversational tone as I addressed the hot topic of discussion across the building, "So, you're a Trump guy, right?"

Nonchalantly, he replied, "No, we see more opportunities with her."

Wait a second… What!? Now, every hair on my body stood on end. What on earth could he have meant by that?

Who Is We and What Opportunities Do You See?

Hang on a second, Colonel, you may be thinking, *people switch sides all the time, right?*

Sure they do, but this guy was a staunch Republican, which is why he was ousted by Obama when he came to office. And to give you context, the majority of party defections go from Blue to Red, not the other way, especially this close to an election. In fact, in 2016, only one senior Republican switched from Red to Blue: William Mundell. Six went the other way, going Red.

As we all know, this was a period of increased political polarization. Battle lines were clearly being drawn between those who supported Crooked Hillary and those who wanted anyone but her. Among the latter, the camp was not as divided as one would think; there was clear consensus within the Pentagon that Trump would win the nomination, despite the attempts of the mainstream media to discredit his candidacy.

So, I was alarmed by the "we" he referenced. He was not alone in this. Who in the world is "we"?

I tensed up, and said, "Who is "we," and what opportunities do you see?" Perhaps louder than I intended. This, coupled with the fire in my eyes, was easy for him to read. Maybe he'd assumed I was in on whatever he was referring to as well?

"Uh… I gotta shoot… see you around, John!" Poof… like that, he was gone, rushing off in the opposite direction.

I stood there for a moment in stunned silence, thoughts of getting to my meeting on time gone from my head. Now, my head was consumed by new thoughts. Dots were connecting, puzzle pieces fitting together, and years of cumulative experiences, eyebrow-raising moments, and suspicions began racing across my mind, pieces falling into place.

At this moment, my life changed. I realized why God had gifted me with the innate knowledge of what I wanted to be from a young age, guiding me down a path that ultimately led to this moment.

Oh my... there is a Deep State, I realized with amazing clarity, *We have a real problem. We can't even trust our own side of the ledger.*

I was horrified that this corruption had infiltrated our military and national security culture, a culture I had put on a pedestal and worshiped, the very center of American military might, intelligence, and strength. I was astonished that it was so brazen. That there was no attempt to hide it. It was so blatant.

I felt betrayed. I felt angry. I learned that everything I'd been fighting for, for my whole life, is corrupted. I asked myself the question, and to this day I still do, who have I been serving? Have I, unwittingly and accidentally, betrayed the citizens of America—the very people I was sworn to protect, serve, and who have paid my wages for my entire working life?

A cacophony of emotions and feelings battled in my head: betrayal, anger, shame, fury, disappointment... and hope. Hope peaked its head. This new knowledge, the clear, irrefutable knowledge that there was a hidden force at work, eroding our sovereignty and freedom, inspired hope within me. Now that I knew my enemy, I could strike back at them, which has led me to where I am now, writing books and appearing on TV, podcasts, and on the news. Being a voice of resistance and change.

In that moment, I swore to action. I said to myself, *We need to reseize control of society and our government. What do we do...?*

Chapter Three
What is the Deep State?

Finally, on both sides of the Atlantic, our citizens are confronted by yet another danger — one firmly within our control. This danger is invisible to some but familiar to the Poles: the steady creep of government bureaucracy that drains the vitality and wealth of the people. The West became great not because of paperwork and regulations but because people were allowed to chase their dreams and pursue their destinies.

Donald Trump – Warsaw, July 2017

I think it is time that I tell you more about the Deep State and how it attacks us every day without us even knowing about it. For some of you reading this book, some of the things I am about to tell you will be nothing new to you. For many more, this will serve as a true eye-opener. A revealing of that mysterious thing you have heard so much about, especially since Donald J. Trump took office.

Now, I will start this chapter by acknowledging up top that not everybody likes Donald Trump. Trump is to conservatives what Obama is to liberals, and both led to distinct divides in American political identities. This is what the Deep State wants. Our division makes them stronger. It prevents tangible opposition from arising and unifying, from moving with a singular purpose.

But, love him or hate him, Trump and his closest advisors openly challenged the Deep State, bringing conversations about them to the mainstream. Strange, isn't it, how these have quieted since Sleepy Joe stole the office?

And Trump did not just do it here, in the US, but he did it on the global stage. Let me take you to Warsaw, in July 2017, just six months after Trump was inaugurated as the 45th President of the United States of America. In front of this global audience, Trump reinforced the American commitment to global security, pledging US support against the spread of authoritarianism and oppression, and reminding the world that America has led this charge throughout the twentieth and twenty-first centuries.

In this speech, he summarized an invisible danger, one wrapped in layers of bureaucracy and red tape, invisible to the naked eye. He correctly identified that Poland, the stage upon which he was standing, was well aware of this threat. They had lived for decades under its most direct manifestation: communism, and in particular, Soviet Communism. Without making this a treatise on the history of Poland, the people of Poland have lived for several hundred years with an assertive and sometimes violent opponent on either side of them that refused to allow a Polish identity.

Trump spoke of the "steady creep of government bureaucracy that drains the vitality and wealth of the people." Vitality and wealth. Energy and prosperity. Sounds an awful lot like slavery, right?

That, ladies and gentlemen, is the end goal of the Deep State, to control the world's resources for the exclusive benefit of an elite few. Obama's "You didn't build that"[2] captures the essence and the flavor of the haughty,

---

2. July 13, 2012, President Obama in Roanoke, VA. Left-leaning fact checkers quibble with this infamous quote endlessly, sorry—taken in context, the president's comment implies government comes first, innovators only exist because of public money. This logic must be flipped and inverted. Yes, the government has a role and can possibly help, but there is an established track record of the government having a negative return on investment (ROI), which for most Americans means the government return for a dollar spent means less than a dollar returned, which means going broke. But those benefiting from the government Disneyland do not care.

imperious attitude of the Deep Staters. In Poland, and across the Soviet Eastern Bloc, the United States and its allies stood in staunch opposition to the USSR and the toppling domino effect of communism through the twentieth century.

Poland knows this better than most. Poland serves as a clear example of the power of the Deep State when it exists in its purest form. You see, the thing about the Deep State is, to the unaware, it has an incredibly alluring appeal. And at the end of the Second World War, when abandoned by its Western allies and saddled with economic debt and societal collapse as a result of a two-fronted invasion, Poland opted to side with the Soviet Union.

The USSR, with amazing success, used Marxist principles to spread lies about a utopian way of living, where everybody works together for the good of the State, and everybody reaps the reward. History has shown that this is not the case.

The new puppet government came in with promises of land reform, an unprecedented rebuilding program aimed at undoing the damage of invasion (of which the Soviet Union had a 50 percent stake, mind you), and a raft of "progressive" social policies. If information was able to flow freely within the Soviet Union, they would have known that this was a lie.

Sure, on the face of it, the initial implementation of these policies looked great, but just as in Stalinist Russia, land reform soon gave way to collectivization, property was requisitioned by the State, and all generated wealth was now exclusively owned by the State, with little social redistribution to be seen.

Artistic license was revoked under strong censorship, and religious affiliation was outlawed—a tough pill to swallow for a strongly Catholic nation—under the Marxist "opiate of the masses" doctrine. Not to mention the pogroms.

This is the true face of the Deep State; this is the "utopia" they are looking for, where people are treated as tools, with the sole aim of working for the State, their labor, and their toil lining the pockets of their wealthy oppressors and leaders.

It is little more than modern slavery.

When the Soviet Union fell, the communist regime in Poland fell with it. Yet still, the influence of the Deep State remains, and it remains in the way that it exists in the United States.

You see, the general public attitude toward communism and declared communists is ostracism. Poland is an ancient country (despite aggressive neighbors), with a proud, Christian heritage, and the communist governments of Poland sought to erode this. As such, they are vilified and hated by the population in general.

Yet still, their influence remains. Former communists have remained active in Polish politics, and in some cases, despite their public vilification, have managed to claw their way to the top of the political pile into national leadership positions, such as in the case of former two-term President Aleksander Kwaśniewski.

Oddly reminiscent of our own questionable electoral system, wouldn't you say?

Cult of the Swamp Narrative

It was against this backdrop that our brave president reminded the world of the threat posed by the Deep State, in a nation that typifies the struggle against it and the influence of it.

Of course, Trump is not the first president to warn of the dangers of the Deep State and to face stern opposition. Reagan did it too.

When Jimmy Carter signed the Civil Service Reform Act of 1978, civil servants flooded the Capitol, and Reagan lamented how Carter's attempt at "professionalizing" the US government actually led to overwhelming union power, processes overladen with bureaucracy, and prioritization with maintaining the status quo as opposed to enacting or allowing any real change.

Reagan also frequently lamented the lack of active opposition to and action against communism, particularly at a time when it seemed that the Bear was wounded and was clearly in its death throes.

Indeed, the Deep State has operated within the CIA for years. It is odd, to me, that an intelligence agency, designed solely to inform and serve the executive actively seeks to manipulate policy and, in many instances, oppose the Reagan Doctrine that sought to supply aid to third-world resisters to communism. Some may say that all of those who stood up for the CIA under the National Security Act of 1947,[3] later amended in 1949,[4] were the original Deep Staters. There is some truth to that, but I would also assert that many were also rock-solid Americans who knew that America was involved in a life-or-death struggle with communism. I invite everyone to review the 1954 Doolittle Report that set the purpose, panache, and bravado the agency needed to implement to protect America and win.[5] I am all for this, but there is one small problem: the American citizen is now the target, and the purpose is to ensure the continuity of the Deep State. Chairman Xi would heartily approve of this behavior.

As such, Reagan was keen on supporting resistance movements in Angola, Afghanistan, and Nicaragua, for example, but stopped short of more extreme groups, making determinations as to where support would be the most beneficial for the populace. Mozambique was one such place where a determination was made.

RENAMO, or the Mozambican National Resistance, was known for its brutality. As such, this was one group that Shultz deemed as ill-suited

---

3. https://catalog.archives.gov/id/299856

4. https://history.defense.gov/Portals/70/Documents/dod_reforms/NSA1947amended1949.pdf

5. https://www.cia.gov/readingroom/docs/CIA-RDP86B00269R000100040001-5.pdf. Report team led by the same legend who flew army bombers off navy aircraft carriers in 1942.

to US support. The CIA, however, felt otherwise and attempted to sway President Reagan to offer aid to RENAMO. They did this by providing false intelligence to the president, exaggerating their military prowess and their popular support, as well as presenting a map that falsely displayed RENAMO as holding most of Mozambique at the time. This was not true.

And this is not the only example. I could show you dozens more examples from southern Africa, Angola, and issues that go well beyond simple misinformation but active sabotage and having direct conversations with insurgent leaders, without the correct lines of approval.

Another interesting example is the Cuban Missile Crisis, where CIA "experts" were adamant that the Soviet Union had not and would not place missiles in Cuba. The CIA Director refused to accept this narrative, and American pilots were placed in danger, with some killed,[6] challenging the mini-Deep State narrative and attitude already forming inside the CIA. This revolt of the mini-Deep State is an important fact that is routinely overlooked when reviewing the history of the Cuban Missile Crisis. In my undergraduate work at the University of Washington, one of my professors was revered as a legend as one of the CIA imagery analysts who saved the world. I now wonder if he was part of the clique who fought any alternative version of the narrative.

These examples may look on the surface contrary to the belief that the Deep State supports communism. The truth is, the Deep State is not particularly picky about what form of authoritarianism, subversion, and control it gets as long as it gets it. Once it has control, it can take care of the rest later.

This is what the Deep State wants. It wants to stifle progress and direct any actual change in very specific directions, ones that serve the few, pushing toward consumerism and globalism. As such, Reagan attempted to limit the

---

6.https://www.history.com/news/the-cuban-missile-crisis-pilot-whose-death-may-have-saved-millions

power of the Deep State by controlling appointments, often appointing people into offices for which they had no endorsements, halting the flow of individual, or indeed group, agendas.

And while Deep State opposition and interference have largely been centered on Republican candidates, Democrats who stray from the line have not been immune to it either. Even Obama, the ultra-liberal commander in chief faced opposition when he attempted to close Guantanamo Bay. Read in this what you will, but the Deep State certainly can and does make use of this offshore, high-security prison, conveniently located within a communist state. This is a position that Lunch Bucket Joe has also taken but has, as of yet, done nothing to that effect. I wonder why? Anything to placate the people, right?

There are thousands of other examples that I could relay to you, but what is evident is that, over time, as the Deep State has grown in strength and numbers, its influence has gotten heavier and heavier, to the point where now it is brazen to those who know what to look for.

What Is It?

By now, there is a wealth of literature available on the web and in print about what the Deep State actually is. Here, I am going to do my best to summarize this for you.

In its simplest terms, the term Deep State is one used to describe a network of unelected bodies, entities, and individuals that influence government. The *Merriam-Webster Dictionary* defines it as "an alleged secret network of especially nonelected government officials and sometimes private entities (as in the financial services and defense industries) operating extralegally to influence and enact government policy."

I'd like to draw you to the term "extralegally" here. This term refers to a lack of legal control, regulation, and authority, essentially meaning that the Deep State is able to operate freely and without regulation. It can, in essence, do what it pleases, and our government has systematically over the years created a system where it is easy for it to do so.

The term found its historical origin in Turkey, where it is a direct translation from the term *derin devlet*. Here, it refers to a State within the State, and in Turkey, to a cabal of political organizations and military figures that have existed since the fall of the Ottoman Empire.

In Turkey, the Deep State is not something that people laugh about or pretend does not exist, where liberals laugh into their vegan cheesecakes while those who look to protect our values and ways of life stand on the pulpit. It has been proven to exist.

Turkish parliamentary investigations at the turn of the century revealed entire departments, intelligence bureaus, and military units that had no official recognition within the national government.

Those bodies, paid for by the state, were acting discretely and covertly from within the halls of the Turkish government, and many undoubtedly still are. Merely revealing the Deep State does not remove, it just slithers from under one rock to another.

Throughout Turkey's post-Ottoman era, this Deep State has operated with severe influence, responsible for a large number of massacres, scandals, and creating links between the Turkish government and organized criminal elements within Turkey who repeatedly attack leftist and minority groups within the country, most notably the Kurds.

The best way to describe the Deep State in this regard then is as a secretive, shadowy organization of extralegal political actors that operate over, under, and within government with often secretive motives, but motives that exclusively serve its members.

Of course, the Deep State is not an exclusively Turkish movement, it is simply easy to describe from the perspective of Turkey because it is widely acknowledged. Its existence is irrefutable, and it pervades everyday life.

The Deep State is a global phenomenon. It is happening everywhere. Canada is a prime example of this. Joe Mebrahtu, a Canadian national interviewed for this book, speaks of the abdication of the responsibility to the governments. He talks about how a historically Catholic province like Quebec has allowed its government to remove its loyalty to God and become increasingly secular, to the extent that all marriages are common law marriages—just one example of where the institution has replaced the church.

As he puts it, "The population has been conditioned and trained to believe that whatever the government says is true." This is reinforced by the media, where the Canadian Broadcasting Company (CBC) has become the mouthpiece of the government. Nobody looks to the community anymore; everything is prescribed by the government, and all faith is put there.

The scale of the task of uprooting them is everywhere, and it has to start somewhere, so why not start in the most influential nation on Earth?

In the US, the Deep State has turned Washington into a Swamp, one which President Trump pledged to drain. It has created a shadow government, a clandestine force that operates behind the scenes, with hands in every pie, and individuals in every office across the mainstream media, the military-industrial complex, and the political arenas all over the country.

It is often referred to as the "establishment," which is why Trump is often referred to as "antiestablishment." His sworn mission, which remains even now that he has been ousted, is to dredge the Swamp, to overturn the establishment. This establishment is a toxic mix of bureaucrats, technocrats, and plutocrats, holding a vast amount of wealth and social influence. They own controlling stakes in so many of the facets that comprise our daily lives. Some would also use the term "uni-party," which I feel has evolved and come true on many accounts. The vote counting debacles in Georgia seem to be a product of collusion between the status quo Republican Party and their "opponents" in the Democrat Party.

If you see it, they've touched it. The phone in your pocket? Check. The stuff you watch on your TV? Check. The news in your feed? Check. The energy that powers your home and keeps the lights on? You betcha! They are everywhere!

And they like things just the way they are. In this world of plenty, they pull all the strings. We are unwittingly subservient to them, we feed into the systems that continue to generate their wealth, their power, and their influence, and so they are doing everything they can to keep it that way.

They do not hold the guns our military owns, but they do own the people who give the orders. Those who sit right at the top of the tree. They continue to advance our technological supremacy because this gives them power not just at home but overseas.

Now imagine the actual good we could do if we cast off their oppression. And please, don't think I'm saying that our soldiers are in on it. They absolutely are not. If you look at those who actively oppose the Deep State, a vast number of them are ex-service personnel. Our troops, our service personnel, are the most loyal of patriots, and so we owe it as much to them to overthrow the tyranny of the Deep State.

The fact is, they are everywhere, pulling at everything from behind the scenes. In their pockets are vast, immeasurable wealth, our politicians, and the blood, sweat, and tears of our people and our children.

They are hell-bent on stripping away your liberty, much like the communists, much like China and North Korea, and as is now more evident than ever, Russia.

So, in summary, the Deep State is essentially the merging of interests to control society on scale by those *"who know what's best for society."* These people are human beings also, but they have joined this bubble of elites who are convinced they know what is best for society.

Who Is It?

As I said earlier, the Deep State is a toxic mix of bureaucrats, technocrats, and plutocrats. Let's break these down in a bit more detail to reveal the true face of the enemy. Doing so will allow you to see clearly the deceit that sits in front of you, how you can stop unwittingly feeding into it, and how you can take action to overturn it.

Bureaucrats: A bureaucrat is someone who works as an official in government. A bureaucrat is concerned with the day-to-day running of government, particularly where it regards procedural correctness and lines of accountability. Often, this comes at the expense of the needs of people, which contributes strongly to the general lack of popularity surrounding bureaucrats within the US.

The job of a bureaucrat, therefore, is to slow things down, which often comes at the expense of change. Now, imagine that impact in a system that has created a whopping 2.8 *million* bureaucrats.

The effect is a state apparatus that no longer cares about the people it serves. Even without the leaders of the Deep State, it has led to a faceless way of operating that focuses on process and policy before the requirements of the people it serves.

A healthy level of bureaucracy is necessary. We have a large population, a vast country with a large number of cultures and demographics, not to mention biomes and environments. Such diversity requires an effective bureaucracy to manage all of that administration.

The problem is that ours is ineffective. It is too big, not to mention that it is corrupt, infiltrated by the leaders of the Deep State. Now, entire wings and sections of the administrative apparatus of our bureaucratic system are devoted to this cause.

And they are able to hide it. They are able to hide it because the system is so massive. Spotting the traitor is like *Where's Waldo?*, only everyone looks exactly like Waldo. They blend in with ease because the very system is designed to be obstructive. And it is not like these people are likely to hold their hands up and declare, "Hey, I'm a traitor!"

To make matters worse, these civil "servants" are protected by civil-service protections, meaning that when political parties change, they do not. They, more often than not, remain in office, giving them the time necessary to grow their influence and cement their influence. In this regard, presidents do not matter.

And this is not even the end of the story, not even close! The actual number of bureaucrats who operate within government departments is larger because of the presence of private contractors. These private contractors are not bound in the same way the government bureaucrats are because they are brought in from external sources.

Who makes the decisions on who comes in? Who determines which private contractors are used? How deep does the corruption actually run? Who do these internal and external contractors actually serve?

Technocrats: When we talk about technocrats, we are not talking about robots and computer screens, at least not yet! In a technocracy, those who lead are not career politicians, they are individuals with a high level of expertise, often technical or scientific.

In governing, this often manifests itself in the form of economists. When the euro was collapsing in 2010, many of the countries at the sharp end of this drop, such as Greece and Italy, turned to technocrats as their saving graces, as their knights in shining armor who would pull them out of their respective crises.

In Italy, the economist Mario Monti was declared prime minister, and in Greece, another economist, Lucas Papademos, took the helm, both charged with steering their countries out of the crises in which they found themselves.

Now, if we pretend for a moment that this was not an engineered crisis, then these appointments were pretty savvy. These guys were not career politicians, they were experts in the field in which their nations were failing.

The problem comes in when these technocrats begin to infiltrate every facet of the government. These people have no real political allegiance. Their allegiance was not to their people but to the problem they were there to fix. But also, in many instances, to the people who put them there.

When I discuss the Four Pillars of Deceit, you'll discover how academia sits central to the system that is designed to maintain the status quo, the system in which the Deep State retains control.

These "intellectuals" are willingly subservient to the Deep State. They are funded by them, given their stipends and their positions because of them, and they serve willingly.

And their presence is growing within the US government. There are hundreds of them in the Pentagon, and they have taken up permanent residence in the Capitol and White House. In such numbers, it is easy for them to sway policy. They are trusted—do not forget, we look to them as trusted experts in our times of need.

Technocracy does not need to be led by a technocrat, as in the examples of Greece and Italy. In many, the leader is a career politician, but they are surrounded on all sides by academic "experts" and their extremely convincing opinions.

Mr. Vaccine himself, Dr. Fauci, is a key example of this. This Chief Medical Advisor to the President has convinced two presidents, and societies at large through bogus science and downright lies, that we all need to pollute our bodies with a vaccine that causes more issues than it solves.

This same "doctor" propagated the over-the-top, hard-line stance on the laboratory-manufactured Chinese virus because doing so meant that when we were all stuck at home, the Deep State had the opportunity to demobilize the Trumpist momentum, take stock, and incite the population toward hatred of the very president who introduced unprecedented tax reform and financial stimuli to help us all weather the storm.

And who emerges as the hero at the end of this storm? Why, it is the Deep State's favorite puppet: election fraud, needle-in-the-arm Corn Pop befriended Joe Biden, capitalizing on the work of the people who came before him and using the "expertise" of the technocrats to justify his actions.

This is the danger of the technocrat, they make subversion and lies sound so appealing and so legitimate. They are key tools in the public-facing machine of the Deep State. They smile at us, convincing us they are right while, behind our backs, they plot the most effective ways to take our freedom.

Plutocrats: A plutocrat is, plain and simple, a person whose power derives from extreme wealth, and in America, we have a lot of these! Hooray for capitalism—no, hooray for "crony capitalism." Crony capitalism is not capitalism, it is favoritism so that the unique innovator or outsider is prevented from rising because they have not conformed to the narratives and goals that all are supposed to be following. A few names spring immediately to mind in regard to the collusion of the wealthy: the Rockefellers, the Rothschilds, the Koches. These family dynasties are in possession of unfathomably vast amounts of influence, business interests, and power to corrupt. After all, wealth buys power, and when your wealth has granted you monopolistic power and influence over a given resource, the world, and in particular the US, has no choice but to take note.

These older dynasties are now being joined by newer ones, those that control information, tech, and media businesses, adding information, dissemination, and technological dependence to a portfolio that already boasted banking and energy. Besides the obvious ways of exerting influence, through that old favorite "donations," or should I say more correctly, bribery, these nefarious actors have even more effective ways of influencing policy and the very ways that we think and absorb information. Bribery, donations, and lobbying are simply the public faces of manipulation.

Behind the scenes, something far more nefarious is happening. The Soros-led media that we consume every day cherry-picks its stories, carefully selecting narratives and individuals that support their stances and agendas while lambasting and satirizing those that stand in opposition.

They convince us that common sense is nonsense and that the only way of thinking—the only set of norms and values that have any values—are theirs. They dictate the flow of public discourse, setting the agendas that the rest of the world blindly follows because they are led to believe that this is what is "right."

And they do this through the gadgets that we use. Their tool, their primary weapon, is globalism. To them, boundaries are a bad thing. Boundaries disrupt the flow of their profits and obstruct the dissemination of the information that they wire into our brains every day. The phones in our pockets remove the physical barriers that exist between societies, making global communication instantaneous.

While there is no doubt that this is an immensely useful tool for all parties, for plutocrats, it means that they can make money from you regardless of where you are. They can feed information to you wherever you may be. They turn you into the product, your information, and your data, and they can track your every movement and thought through GPS tracking and your search history.

And we thank them for it. We throw a salute to globalism because it seemingly makes our lives easier.

If ever you feel like questioning the power of a plutocracy, look at the severe global impact of the invasion of Ukraine by Russia. In fact, just look at the realization of an oligarchical society in Russia, where former upper-echelon communists monopolized all of the essential industries within the nation and propped up the world's most dangerous dictator after the Chinese Communist Party leader because he keeps the money flowing. These people wield absolute power, indefatigable global influence, and have remained unimpacted by some of the most severe sanctions aimed at individuals in history.

Worried yet? Scared yet? I am not here to make you feel afraid. Believe it or not, my objective is to give you hope. Now, though, it seems I have given myself an uphill task. I have revealed to you, by way of a very quick summary (I could write many books on this subject alone, and many have already been written) of the true extent of Deep State corruption in the United States.

I have detailed the brevity of the influence of the Deep State and the all-encompassing influence that they have on all of our lives. And I know this is depressing to hear. It is hard to hear, and it is hard to imagine how we defeat this or prevent it from owning us without locking ourselves away in some cave in the middle of a desert, disconnecting ourselves from the world like a staff-bearing hermit.

But now that you know the extent of the influence and the sheer size and scope of the Deep State, you hopefully now realize that there is no way to defeat them from the top. Trump tried, he exposed the truth to us all, and look what happened there; they simply stole the White House.

Hopefully, if you did not before, you now realize the truth in my assertion that the only way to defeat the Deep State is at the local level. We, the people, have to create an inescapable tide of momentum that, as it gathers pace, washes away the power and influence of the Deep State and returns it to the loyal citizens of our great Republic.

Part Two

Chapter Four

I Know They Exist, Here's How

my century… is unique in the history of men for two reasons. It is the first century since life began when a decisive part of the most articulate section of mankind has not merely ceased to believe in God, but has deliberately rejected God. And it is the century in which this religious rejection has taken a specifically political form….

Whittaker Chambers

Who am I to tell you all about the Deep State? What is it that gives me the knowledge, and therefore the ability, to talk to you all in such confidence about what the threat is, who operates from the shadows, and how to defeat them?

I suppose, then, it is time to introduce you to me. My name is Colonel (Ret.) John Mills. I am the former Director of Cybersecurity Policy, Strategy, and International Affairs at the Department of Defense, and a fellow at the Center for Security Policy. I have lived a long career serving the United States of America, from active and reserve service in the US Army, fighting on battlefields all over the world, to advising presidents, secretaries of defense, and senior policymakers in the Pentagon, the White House, and Capitol Hill.

I have done this across five eras of US foreign and domestic policy: the Cold War, the Peace Dividend, the War on Terror, the World in Chaos, and now the Great Power Competition. I have devoted my life to serving the people of the United States, and I have done it with pride and with honor.

I have not always fought against the Deep State, and I am ashamed to admit that, due to my career (of which I am exceedingly proud), I have likely unwittingly and accidentally promoted the interests of various elements of the Deep State. It was not until that encounter in the "A" Ring that I knew and understood what Donald J. Trump coined as the "Deep State."

Throughout the years, I have had many experiences of which I am immeasurably proud, and others that at the time caused me to raise my eyebrows as I questioned what was going on around me. Over the years, my suspicions grew, though what I was suspicious about for a long time was unclear to me.

It was during my time serving in Virginia and Washington that things began to click, and that encounter in the "A" Ring was my moment of illumination, the moment that all of the pieces came together to cast a burning light on the secret forces that operate within the shadows.

It should tell you something that I, a loyal patriot, a dedicated serviceman, and former employee of the US government to which I committed myself so devoutly, have performed a full about-face and have adopted a staunch stance against the establishment. I am loyal to the Constitution, but not this version of it in the current US government. I am loyal to a government that serves its people in totality, forsaking the interests of those who have worked for decades to infiltrate and operate a State within a State.

That government does not exist in current times. I am loyal to an idea that, at this moment in time, does not exist, but that I, and so many millions of others, are fighting tooth and nail to restore.

I refuse to let them win, and I proudly consider myself a revolutionary soldier who is willing to lay down his life to defend his country, as I have done my whole life up to now.

The Original Deplorable

As I reflect on who I am and what I have gone through, it resembles the Whittaker Chambers experience. Whittaker Chambers outed the insidious nature and representation of communism. A lot of people in elite society would harrumph at the bringing up of the name Whittaker Chambers, but he was right, and he was justifiably posthumously honored with the Medal of Freedom by President Reagan.

What Whittaker Chambers and I share is vehement opposition to communism. We also share our steadfast conviction in faith. Whittaker Chambers often lamented the state of faith in the Western World, which he deemed as causal to the domino effect of cascading communism. In his book, *Witness*, Whittaker Chambers revealed the parallels and the intimate relationship between God and freedom:

"Religion and freedom are indivisible. Without freedom the soul dies. Without the soul there is no justification for freedom. Necessity is the only ultimate justification known to the mind. Hence every sincere break with Communism is a religious experience, though the Communist fails to identify its true nature, though he fails to go to the end of the experience. His break is the political expression of the perpetual need of the soul whose first faint stirring he has felt within him, years, months or days before he breaks. A Communist breaks because he must choose at last between irreconcilable opposites—God or Man, Soul or Mind, Freedom or Communism."

God is final. There is much we can do to fight the good fight, but without faith in God, it is not a fight that we can win. God gives us courage, God gives us strength, and God gives us the most American of ideals… freedom.

There is a reason that so many pastors have joined this fight and are leading from the front. They know the threat that the Deep State poses to global worship and faith in God. There is a satanist element to all of this, but we will save that for another time.

What Chambers and I do not have in common is that he started out as a communist. Drawn to communism by a difficult upbringing and tough familial relationships, he believed he found a community within which he was welcome.

He acted as an agent of communism, conducting espionage activities on the US government on behalf of the Soviet regime, and would deservedly be strung up for treason had he not defected and conducted the same espionage but on behalf of the United States.

Stalin's purges shook his faith in communism, and the unholy alliance between the Reds and the Nazis sealed by the Molotov–Ribbentrop Pact in August 1939 confirmed his suspicions—communism was evil and was forming evil alliances.

As a result, he revealed a network of spies and agents operating within the US government and participated in trials to convict these communists, most notably in the Hiss trial.

Faith is forbidden within communism. Faith detracts from the belief in the State and leads to a moral conviction that makes watching the atrocities of communism unbearable. This was the case with Chambers; he joined the communist movement out of a genuine belief that it would benefit humanity, and when he discovered the truth, he turned to faith and used faith as his weapon with which to fight communism throughout and after the Second World War. And it worked.

This time in American history is known as the Red Scare, and despite what the naysayers may tell you, it was an important chapter in American post–World War Two history. In school, we were most likely told about the

Red Scare from the Howard Zinn point of view: that it was evil and there was no Red Scare.

There WAS a Red Scare. There were communists infiltrating governments all over the world. We have the proof; we have the convictions. So why do so many people reject the possibility of infiltration in our government today, at a time where it can be done both in person and from afar, through the use of technology, and viruses… communication is instant. The infiltrators no longer need shady overcoats, wide-brimmed hats, and secret landline phone calls. They can simply tap their screens and commit treason instantly.

These are the same people who now say there is a Russian behind everything in the world, falsely claiming that Trump colluded with a Russian government that he so publicly criticized and opposed. Wait, if that were true, where were you during the Cold War?

The Clinton release of the Venona Tapes in the '90s[7] provided a lot of factual evidence that people accused of being communists were, guess what? Actually communists.

What Chambers and I have in common is that we both operated from within the power that we now seek to destroy. We both witnessed firsthand the corruption that became our lives' missions to overthrow.

My exposure to the inner workings of American politics gives me the perfect insight to tear away the shroud and remove the pieces of the machine that make the Deep State tick. The Deep State is to me what communism was to Whittaker Chambers—an evil that strips away our freedom and demands servitude under the guise of utopia.

We are also united in our faith, in our belief that God is the final answer, that our enemies are godless, and that it is faith that gives us a strength that

---

7. https://www.nsa.gov/Helpful-Links/NSA-FOIA/Declassification-Transparency-Initiatives/Historical-Releases/Venona/

the Deep State does not possess. God is our rallying call. He is the banner under which we should all unite. The Bible is the only truth, and Psalm 9:9 tells us that: "The LORD also will be a refuge for the oppressed, a refuge in times of trouble."

And with the Bible being the final truth, the great betrayers would do well to remember that "He that oppresseth the poor to increase his riches, and he that giveth to the rich, shall surely come to want."[8] It is not just the plutocrats and the technocrats who shall meet their reckoning, but their bureaucrats too; those that make their ambitions reality.

Dinner in London

In the immediate aftermath of that momentous encounter in the "A" Ring, my mind raced. I spent hours revisiting key moments of my life and career, events that solidified my love for this country alongside events that shook my faith in its government and its inner workings.

During this period of reverie, reflection, and awakening, I want to take you to another occasion, shortly after, where many of my fears were confirmed.

It was early October 2016. Election campaigning was in full swing, and Trump and his campaign team were in full swing revealing the crimes committed and the lies told by Crooked Hillary during her ill-fated time as secretary of state. (Somehow, she got away with squirreling away tens of thousands of emails, right into the hands of her Deep State coconspirators.) Former President Obama took thousands and thousands of pages away from the White House with a promise to digitize, and yet the National Archives has never seen these documents again. And yet we now have a historic inflection point in American history with the weaponized and corrupt FBI and DOJ raiding President Trump's house. A shameful day that has changed America forever.

---

8. Proverbs 22:16 KJV

At this time, my office was with the Pentagon, but I had three parts of the Department of Defense cyber portfolio.

1. **Policy:** These are the DOD directives and instructions on cyber security. Pretty boring stuff, but it makes the DOD run. This stuff will "put hair on your chest." It is the stuff that is not normalized; you're getting "N+1" stuff that is not normalized. Because it is not normalized, it has not been taken care of at a lower level. So when you are in the Office of the Secretary of Defense or at the Joint Staff, you always have to be on your toes because you are always being handed things that do not quite fit or are new and unsolved. I had a number of employees quit or ask to be reassigned because they could not handle the chaos of the senior-level decision-making world.

A lot of people think that when you work at the pinnacle, everything is calm... serene, and you have all the time in the world to sip your coffee and think big thoughts.

It is the exact opposite.

2. **Strategy:** This is where documents were written at the White House level, the interagency (agreed upon promulgations of multiple US government departments and agencies,) and the Department of Defense to articulate the intent, the direction, and the people, programs, and resources needed to carry out these strategies. This included issuances such as the 2011 DOD Strategy for Operating in Cyberspace, but also large programs such as the Comprehensive National Cybersecurity Initiative, started by Bush ("W"), reviewed, endorsed, and doused with gasoline (i.e., additional budget and scope) by the Obama team.

3. **International Affairs:** My job was to service signed information-sharing agreements between the DOD and key international

partners and also seek updates to these agreements or establishment of new agreements. Basically, these agreements were simply partner nations saying, *I give you something, and you give me something back*; that's what information sharing is. As a result, I spent a lot of time talking to foreign officials on behalf of the United States all over the world.

My position was such over the years that I worked on the creation of the Comprehensive National Cybersecurity Initiative (CNCI), and at one point, I recall being informed that I was on the Top 100 list for the state security of a foreign power and later that I was likely on the ISIS list of targets. Needless to say, I was deeply involved in the inner workings of our state security, and this made me a target and, at the very least, a person of interest for many of the enemies of our nation.

I loved this job, which made the thoughts swirling around my head all the more difficult to bear, comprehend, and reconcile. Working with the secretary of defense meant that I felt an overwhelming duty to protect American interests and the interests of the American people. I had also worked in the Joint Chiefs of Staff and in the halls of the Eisenhower Executive Office Building at the National Security Council up to this point, so I had been exposed to the pinnacles of civilian leadership and the uniform leadership of the DOD and the entire US government.

Working in these departments means that you have to be on your A-game, especially if you are working across these two staffs, the White House, other departments and agencies, and key foreign partners as I often was. The players in this environment really are, in many ways, the best of the best, and you will either get run over and fired, lose your mind or excel.

I had, over the years, between thirty and fifty people working for me, a crack team of support staff that helped keep my operation running. Staff had to be among the best of the best, and we had what are called integrees from the intelligence community who were looking to fulfill their JDA, or Joint Duty Assignment, qualifications.

On top of this, you had your support contractors; these had to be your A-plus support contractors, the very best people you could get your hands on. Needless to say, we were surrounded by the very best people, and people who were going to rise to the top.

I joined this office in 2004 from the Joint Chiefs of Staff. What got me in this office was my planning, organizing, and implementing skills in the chaos of when the CNCI[9] program took off in 2007.

I was very good at making order out of chaos, a skill that years in the military refines in you, and CNCI was chaos on a grand scale. It was a program that started with the best of intentions to up the American game on cybersecurity but essentially set the framework and the pathway to spying on American citizens and the president on a grand scale. So what I unintentionally helped to create were some of the key programs and tools used to collect data on a president, a presidential candidate, and American citizens. Remember what I said unwittingly about accidentally helping the enemy…

My NSA boss (I was not NSA) who was detailed to the secretary of defense saw my work, liked what I did, and pulled me over.

With this coming so close to another election, I was put straight from the frying pan into the fryer, and I had to quickly learn on the job. Luckily, this office was not too dissimilar from the Joint Chiefs, so I was able to integrate and assimilate quickly. The key difference is that the Joint Chiefs are the A-team of the uniform world, and the entire DOD is a civilian-run agency, not a military-run agency.

Which seems odd, right? That the apparatus that controls our military is not, in itself, military. Well, the Goldwater-Nichols Act of 1986 mandated

9. https://obamawhitehouse.archives.gov/issues/foreign-policy/cybersecurity/national-initiative

and made it absolutely clear that the Department of Defense was civilian-run to prevent generals from running amok and doing their own thing, pulling all matters military firmly from the realm of the elected government. Goldwater-Nichols was essentially democratically sound, but making it all too easy for the Deep State to ooze its way in.

Back to 2016, and on October 4 I believe it was, I was on a commercial flight to London for a Five Eyes meeting. This was part of a package of three meetings, first to London for a Five Eyes meeting, then a flight from London to Singapore to meet with the Singaporean Ministry of Defense, then to Hawaii to meet with the Taiwanese Ministry of Defense in a first of a kind meeting, then back to Washington, DC.

The leg that gave me a bit of concern was the leg from London to Singapore. This was about two years after Malaysian Airlines Flight 17 was shot down over Ukraine. It took me a while to figure out the flight that met the Joint Travel Regulations yet avoided the ongoing battle areas of Ukraine as much as possible. It took me a while, but I finally figured out a route that met the JTR and minimized the surface-to-air missile exposure over Ukraine battle areas—not the first time I faced concerns during a flight. I experienced an in-flight engine fire in a C-141 and in another episode, possibly the same Royal Air Force C-130 I flew into Baghdad International in 2003 went down in Iraq in January 2005. This RAF C-130 loss was and still is a national scandal in the United Kingdom.

On the first leg of the flight, I was joined, seemingly coincidently at the time, by someone I had sat across from at many of the meetings at the Eisenhower Executive Office Building during the creation and implementation of the CNCI initiative. He was retired from government service and now working for a growing cybersecurity firm. It was good to see him and a couple of other people I recognized on the flight, including a retired general I had worked very closely with.

This was a trip between the capitals of two of the closest and trusted partners in the world, so seeing others in government service was not unusual on such flights.

I was intrigued and excited by this; this person was a figure I respected, trusted, and admired, and I looked forward to spending some time talking with him during the trip and the line through customs. He is very well-liked in the current and retired federal law enforcement community, and at the time, to the best of my knowledge, he was just performing his post-government duties and obligations to his company. (I know, I still did not fully understand or know about Deep State then, even though I had received my life-changing Taser jolt in the "A" Ring less than ninety days previously.) Upon reflection, I realize now that he was almost certainly sent at the behest of Comey to accelerate the Crossfire Hurricane operation that was swirling only thirty days out from the election.

As we slowly proceeded together through the long line through British entry procedures at Heathrow, I asked him, "What brings you to London?"

Although we talked about many things, I never quite received an answer on the reasons for his flight to London. As far as any mission reasons to London, my question would be answered by a "…Ah, this and that," "Certainly not for the weather," or, "Hey did you see about…"

We said our farewells and went our separate ways after passing through British Customs and retrieving our bags. It was good to see him, and I remember fondly the several years together trying to implement one of the largest interagency programs in American post–World War II history in the largest bureaucracy in the world. He had also rendered vital assistance to me during a trip to China several years earlier, something for which I was eternally indebted to him for his assistance. As I saw him depart, it left a good feeling, and I wondered when our paths would cross again.

Well, that question was answered a couple of nights later when I joined a dinner given by a common friend of ours, and there he was again. After predinner socializing with a group of fifty or so Hillary-leaning elitists, a second life-changing jolt awaited me.

Palace Intrigue

There is always palace intrigue going on in DC—clandestine, closed-door meetings, sudden unexpected opportunities to retrofit meetings and lobby or talk personal and political agendas. The Deep Staters excel at this, and this "meeting" would be no different. Prior to my Five Eyes meeting, I was invited to a dinner that, coincidentally, my friend and unexpected traveling partner would also be attending. This invite was passed along to me by the organizer, a friend, and someone whom I now consider to be "one of us," an ally in the fight against the Deep State.

And to alleviate any worries you may have about the organizer, I can tell you categorically that he is one of us, that he is on our team. He himself is a retired member of senior federal law enforcement, so he has been witness to things that would make you tremble, seen firsthand the extent and the depravity of the Deep State, and he now deals with a lot of the Big Tech circles. He knows well that you have to be careful in that crowd because it leans heavily for the Deep State government.

What makes me sick about this dinner is that, at the time, I still did not totally know what the Deep State actually was, but just like Whittaker Chambers, I was in it, and somebody I had great respect for would reveal himself to be one of the "high priests" of the Deep State.

I had been invited to this dinner coincidentally—I had never been to one of these in London before, so I did not know what to expect. I remember walking into this grand room with over thirty other people, red-backed, golden gilded chairs, a fancy menu, which I took a picture of to show my daughter (I figured she would be jealous of the food, she loves to eat the same stuff I do!), and took my seat at the same table as my now former friend and traveling companion.

I remember feeling pretty excited, looking forward to having some real enlightening conversations with some pretty influential people, at least until the opening icebreaker, where everyone reveals what their passion is. Turns out, a lot of people have a passion for lying and treason.

Instead of enlightening conversations and strategic networking, the only strategies I saw being formed were those that were whispered between huddled backs and under cupped hands. The room was abuzz with the whispers of those who did not want to be heard, whose words were dangerous. I am not talking about every individual in the room, but it was enough to get my attention.

I was like a fish out of water. There were some familiar faces, people I recognized, but nobody I truly knew, with the exception of my traveling companion.

What I did know was that many of the faces I saw were Hillary supporters. I was one of a very small number of Trump supporters in the room. And I was okay with that. I am not above having dinner with the opposition, and I try not to judge people by their political affiliation. We all have reasons for supporting who we support, as long as they are the right reason: for the benefit of the nation.

So, we broke the ice and introduced ourselves. These were only meant to be quick introductions, there were over fifty people in the room, but it seemed my "friend," the man I traveled with, did not get the memo.

He stood, introduced himself, and like a Hollywood characterization of what a senior law enforcement official should be like, he ranted to the room.

"Trump is a traitor! He is a Russian asset, is being groomed by Putin for a position at the top, and represents the greatest threat to national security the United States has ever seen. And we're going to prove it!" I stiffened in my chair, taken aback by this outburst. Never, at any stage in our journey, did he give any indication that this was his plan. But in that moment, it clicked in my mind as to why he never revealed to me his reason for traveling. I guess I had found it.

As he dove into his highly unusual tirade, I was shocked to see several people lean forward into their chairs, for the first time in the evening paying rapt attention to what was being said.

The thing about this guy is that he is engaging. He adopted a character that was over-the-top and completely unlike his usual face and used it. Maybe I was seeing him with the mask off, a mask that he had clearly worn for years as he hid his true allegiances.

He was well suited to it. In addition to being a part of a major new start-up in the relevant market space, he had appeared on news venues and other media several times, so he was suited to performing when needed and had clearly rehearsed this song and dance that he presented.

I sat in stunned disbelief as he ranted in true Jim Comey fashion, pointing, shouting, and waving as he spewed his hyperpartisan delusional diatribe at the room. He was overly emotional, vitriolic, and it was too much even for this room of Hillary supporters. Sure, there were some nodding along, but for most, they looked as blown back as I did. Most of the room was confused—Hillary was a sure thing to win, what was this bloke shouting about? Remember, at this time, the "Russian Narrative" was not well-known, circulated, or referenced. But we were all being presented a sneak preview. Few, if any, of us knew how special this performance was.

"...and that, ladies and gentlemen, is why we cannot allow Donald Trump into the White House!" he declared to a weak spattering of applause followed by a stunned awkward silence.

Later, as I did the timeline forensics, I suspected that his reason for being in London was to coordinate stories on Fusion GPS and further spread the lie that the Deep State has been telling since before Trump took office, despite a complete lack of evidence since. It must tell you something when even the most sophisticated network of liars and thieves could not provide any evidence—real or fabricated—to prove it.

I also believe that he still possessed high-level security clearances from the US government and that he and the CIA station chief in London at the time, Gina Haspel,[10] would be meeting to talk about things at a high level of classification. Maybe this was how he found out about this dinner, how he wrangled himself an invite. I do not believe that the organizer would have willingly invited him if he had known that a Deep State plant would be in attendance, but then again, both of us only had a nascent understanding of the scope and depth of the Deep State at this time.

What I do believe is that God was upon this trip. I believe it was God that led to my unanticipated invite, to be on the same flight as my former "friend," to be in London at this time and that this dinner was held at this time, separate from my reason for being there.

I left this dinner with the same resolve that I had left the "A" Ring with, only this time, with fewer questions. I was sent there to witness, firsthand, the blatant and open treason of the Deep State and its puppets, and this dinner confirmed many of the suspicions that had developed over the months prior. I had a clear vision of my enemy, of their tactics, and plans began to swirl in my mind.

---

10. Gina C. Haspel - CIA Career Timeline, 1 May 2018.pdf

Chapter Five

Stop Trump

Today's ceremony, however, has very special meaning, because today we are not merely transferring power from one administration to another, or from one party to another, but we are transferring power from Washington, DC, and giving it back to you, the people.

Donald Trump, 2017 Inauguration Speech

On the evening of Trump's election, I had to go to bed early. The next day, come what may, was going to be tumultuous, and everybody who worked in the Office of the Secretary of Defense was going to be needed to manage the storm, and I needed to get to work early.

My family stayed up to watch the election, and I told my daughter, "If Trump wins, come wake me up. Otherwise, don't wake me," I said a little prayer and headed off to bed.

Instead of the excited shaking I'd hoped for, I was instead awoken by the buzz of my alarm at 3:45 a.m. (which is, yes, my normal time of waking.) *Well, I guess Hillary won.*

My mood was as dark as the inky black sky of that cold November morning. Hillary must have won; nobody had come to wake me. I took a moment to brace myself for the disappointment before I left my bed for a much-needed coffee.

As I emerged from the door of our bedroom, I looked down through the balcony, and I spotted my wife and daughters sleeping, cuddled up on the sofa with the television still on and turned to Fox, of course (at the time, still an impartial station). This, at least, lifted my spirits a little. I smiled at the image.

And my spirits soared when I saw the headline emblazoned on the TV. There, in big bold writing, was the headline:

TRUMP WINS!

My heart leaped! I could not believe it! Donald J. Trump, whom so many believed could not possibly win, was to be the 45th President of the United States! Finally, we would have someone with the courage to "drain the Swamp," tackle the bureaucracy of Washington, and attack the Deep State!

"Guys! Wake up! He did it! Thank God, he did it!" I yelled as I ran down the stairs, nearly tripping on the final few as I ran.

They sprang into life. "Oh, thank you, God! We fell asleep! I can't believe we missed it!" My wife cried, as my daughters hurled themselves across the room and into my arms. My son, awakened by the clamor, came out of his room also and came quickly down the stairs to join us.

"I'm so sorry! I promised that I would come get you!"

"Don't you worry, sweetie, this is not a day to be sorry!" I reassured my eldest daughter through laughter. I will fondly remember this as one of the best mornings of my life, just behind the first morning after my wedding, the morning after the birth of our son, and the beautiful "gotcha" days for our two girls. The shouting, screaming, and excited chatter continued right up to me leaving and my girls took themselves off to bed.

That morning, back in the "A" Ring, I saw the senior assistant to Ash Carter coming toward me looking shell-shocked, devoid of life. I could not help myself.

"Good morning!" I said cheerily, shooting him a big smile and a wave.

"Yeah…morning, John…," he mumbled, half raising his hand and avoiding eye contact as he shuffled past me. The rumor was that if Hillary had won, he would become the Director of the NSA and the Cyber Command would be split off to be a separate Four Star Command. Within days, the Obama Administration was attempting to fire Admiral Mike Rogers, dual-hatted as Director of the NSA and the Commander of Cyber Command, as he rightfully broke the chain of command to warn Donald J. Trump of the initial moves of the post-election coup.

This is interesting because the unmasking and monitoring were taking place at the NSA, which included a sophisticated operation dedicated to the monitoring of Trump personnel. This means that if Hillary had won, he would have been in charge of the organization and all the files and records of all this spying on Trump, meaning that he could have had great influence over whether those files and records were maintained or not.

I always tried to be nonpartisan in the workplace. This, I always found, was the best way to harbor positive relationships and get things done. And like I said, I do not judge people on whether they are Republican or Democrat, only on their moral conviction.

To this extent, I always thought that he had done some good things, so as he passed me, I had a moment's regret at my, perhaps, exuberant early morning hail to this person. I truly meant it at the time and said, "I really hope you're able to stay on. You've done some great things, and your work has been very impactful."

"Yeah… Thanks, John," he replied through a sheepish smile and shuffled off.

Later, I realized as I ran the forensics timeline and who was doing what at what time that he was uniquely suited and positioned to possibly be the quarterback or perhaps even the maestro of Spygate.

Comey, Brennan, and ICA Lies

The next couple of days went by briskly and positively. New faces, loyal faces, began to appear in offices, on email chains, and preparations were made for the transition of power, like they always had been, regardless of the outcome. After all, *we were all professionals, right?* We all swore an oath of office in both uniform and civil service, and to me and others in more nonpartisan days, this was a holy and sacred vow. Things were relatively normal from a transition state, that is until I received a call on the top-secret phone within a few days of the election.

I cannot go into too much detail on the contents of the call for obvious reasons, but key among the topics discussed was the creation of a new interagency working group dedicated to establishing and finalizing the "Trump is a Russian asset" narrative. The caller was eager, exuberant, and excited. The purpose of this spin-up was not just the Russia story—but even better—if we were successful, we would be able to delay, postpone, or call off the inauguration of Donald J. Trump.

I put my head in my hands, thinking, *You gotta be kidding me…* I could not believe what I was hearing. This, barely a month removed from the dinner in London where this dangerous narrative was trundled out with such furious passion. These figures were also connected. The enemy was mobilizing.

This group, led personally by Jim Comey (another link) and John Brennan, spun up and produced what was called the Intelligence Community Assessment, or the ICA, that would be released in January 2017. It was part of my job to help write and then perform the DOD review of this ICA.

When I received the final top-secret package from the interagency group, the document was a dud. I read the whole thing, the whole top-secret document, top to bottom. There was absolutely nothing in there that provided even a shred of evidence or factual support that Trump is, or ever was, a Russian asset.

I laughed when I thought of the line, "there are dinosaurs in this dinosaur park?" when carefully reviewing the document. (There is information about solid, personal Trump collusion with Russia in this purported, "Trump is a Russian Asset" document, right? I wanted to know what I had missed, what I was not aware of, and the evidence that Trump was a Russian asset.)

The Executive Summary of the ICA asserted a Russian connection, but then proffered scant support in the body of the document. Having done literally hundreds of action memos for different secretaries of defense and chairmen of the Joint Chiefs, as well as presidential matters, I handled this review professionally and focused strictly on the facts presented. With no facts being presented, my recommendation for the current secretary of defense was "nonconcur." However, when I presented the action memo and the recommendation to my senior manager for presentation to the secretary of defense, my recommendation was disregarded.

I was outraged! How could this be? I had specifically and clearly explained how this ICA could in no way support such an assertion.

"Uh—what happened here?" I asked, curious but also not very happy as to how an exhibit with no evidence could be approved.

"John," she calmly explained, as we were spinning simultaneously on several topics and about to walk out her office door to another meeting, "no need to staff this any further. The chief of staff has already procured the secretary of defense's signature of concur because Comey and Brennan are personally, hands on keyboard, writing this ICA and executive summary, let's move on to the other topics of the day." And to her, that was that.

To me, this was even more troubling. Their hands were personally on the keyboard typing the executive summary, which is a major red flag: you never EVER get the directors of agencies like the CIA and the FBI personally typing the executive summaries. This would be like if the president was personally writing an action memo; it just never happens. That is what you have staff for, so what was going on here?

In the summer and fall of 2020, when Rick Grennell and John Ratcliffe declassified documents, it was made clear that Comey and Brennan knew the Russia story was fake and was created by Fusion GPS and the Clinton campaign. Yet, as soon as Trump won, they jumped into hyperspeed and produced an ICA that they knew was fake. They were knowingly having staffs across the US government review a fake document.

News flash—this is a big deal and unprecedented in my experience or knowledge of a plethora of staffing actions for some of the most sensitive matters. After seeing the declassifications by Grennell and Ratcliffe, I realized that dozens of senior federal officials, including myself, had been tricked by the Comey/Brennan fraud. And so far, all it has received is a big "Ho-Hum."

False statements by a federal official are a felony under Title 18 of the United States Code, so how have they never been punished? The proof is there, and the direct line of responsibility never gets more direct than this!

As John Edwards said in the 2004 campaign, "There are two Americas." John Edwards was prescient and absolutely spot-on. There are two Americas—one for the Deep Staters and the elite, and one for everyone else.

Finding Top Cover

For the next two years, I worked tirelessly to serve the nation and protect it from internal and external threats, but the truth is, the subversion, undermining, and vociferous lying continued, and what I saw can only be described as crazy. In all my years in government and in public service, I had never seen anything quite like it. I saw careerists undermine Bush W., even Obama a little bit, but now it was open season to stop the Trump Administration. Even "Never Trumpers" hidden as Trump appointees were giving it their best shot.

Throughout these next two years, I developed and acquired all the confirmation and evidence I needed to convince myself of the great lie, the great deception that is happening and has been happening for decades within the US government.

I did not just sit on this information. I tried, repeatedly and often, to do something about it, to take some kind of affirmative action, and found the velocity of the chaos of the coup was making even the simple impossible. Senate and House staff were interested, but actions that would lead to DOJ referrals for prosecution would not appear until the street theater of the contrived "J6" committee, where dangerous economists like Dr. Peter Navarro were arrested at airports. Yes, there are elements of the Stasi in modern-day America. And they operate with the same level of secrecy and espionage.

In early 2017, I tried to talk to the White House about people who I felt were actively and unlawfully undermining Trump. I felt I had made serious ground when a senior assistant to Vice President Pence wanted to see my list. I was overtly aware that an email like that could be grossly misconstrued, so I asked for a face-to-face meeting, but it never happened.

I gave information to the Department of Defense Inspector General's Office, the Department of Justice Inspector General, House and Senate members, and committee staffs. I passed information to anyone for whom it was lawful, compliant, and relevant.

But for all my attempts, it seemed as if nothing was happening with this information. It was going nowhere.

I was also concerned about who I gave information to for a couple of reasons. Firstly, I did not know who to trust. As each day passed, I was increasingly concerned about the rampant corruption I was surrounded by. I had a list of names that I was ready to submit, alongside an ever-growing dossier of incriminating evidence, but I was concerned that if I handed this over, I would be revealing my hand to the wrong person or that this information would simply disappear.

I also knew that if I could not justifiably present evidence from a position that would be in violation of federal law, the Deep State would pounce and use it immediately to bury the information and discredit me in a political version of their favorite media trick: catch and kill. This was something that I knew happening across government.

I had to tread a careful line. There is a distinct difference between whistleblowing and sharing lists of names and other information across departments and agencies—especially where it regards the White House. We have all seen what happens to whistleblowers, and I know how much these covert enemies of the state would love to tar me with the same brush that has ensnared US government whistleblowers and personalities like Julian Assange. To serve your country, you have to know the system—this is one of the first things I tell people who are looking for help in their own personal fights against corruption.

Know the system and use it against them because they will use it against you.

You have to be sensitive about sharing what could be considered law enforcement sensitive or what should be an Inspector General submission. Unbeknownst to me, a patriot by the name of Rich Higgins simultaneously came up with a list of names, many of whom were on my radar, and went straight to POTUS with it.

In his list, he pointed at senior media figures, Islamists, several Black Lives Matter activists, the ACLU, the UN, and several well-known Marxists. He pointed out that, despite their vast differences, these groups and individuals were coordinating together to oppose and undermine the Trump Administration through a process of delegitimization and subversion. Classic tactics, and the very ones I was trying to avoid being the victim of.

Rich was in the privileged position of working in the White House, while I was four miles away in the DOD at the Pentagon, no longer in regular attendance at White House meetings. As a result, he was able to talk directly to the president, whereas I was limited to sending my information electronically, and sending it electronically is vastly different from speaking to someone in person armed with a dossier.

Problem is, anything sent electronically becomes "official government records," unless of course you go down the route of Hillary and do everything from a private server, but I was not about to commit a felony, and I did not want my information to be boxed, warehoused, and forgotten like the final warehouse scene of Indiana Jones and the "Top People," who were the "oh so accurate" Deep Staters, to come along. How prescient this movie was.

What is frightening, and also illuminating, is that despite the fact that he worked at the White House and I worked in the Pentagon for the Department of Defense, we were seeing exactly the same things, and there were some clear similarities and dotted lines, sometimes even bold ones, between the figures on each of our lists.

Later, I did meet and compare notes with Rich. It was an honor to know him and an honor to attend his funeral only a short time ago. His loss is a huge one, not just for his family and those who loved him but for the nation. When all is said and done, Rich will be remembered as a hero.

I endured another two years of what should have been the most productive climax of my career. The problem was, I was still suffering from the handicaps I had been subject to and the damage that my career had endured during the Obama years, and now I was hampered by bureaucratic hurdles and deliberate attempts to stifle progress. I find it a miracle that President Trump got as much done as he did when he was tackling corruption and opposition from within his own party, not to mention the nefarious actors that sit behind the scenes. This was a frustrating period for all.

I did my best to alert those whom I could trust, but an opportunity came in late 2017 for me to retire and continue the fight. From this point forward, this was to be from outside the government. In February 2018, I retired from the US government and sought new approaches to continue the fight and expose the ongoing coup against Trump.

And then, Pelosi and her cronies pushed for impeachment—impeachment based almost wholly on two Deep Staters who broke their oaths of office and became partisan combatants. I'm referring to Eric Ciaramella of the CIA and Alex Vindman, Army Lieutenant Colonel detailed to the Executive Office of the President (along with his twin brother).

Just recently I landed at Dulles Airport and as the Mobile Lounge (often called "Moon Buggies") drove us back to the main terminal, I heard a voice behind me. And who was it?

The same fake source who lied and colluded with the Democrats.

How was that for history? An operative of the Deep State who worked to undermine a president was behind me at the airport named for a man who ran the State Department while his brother ran the early CIA.

As I sought avenues from which to bring the fight, a powerful DC law firm offered to handle my case concerning the adverse impact on my career under Obama. They were going to take it on 100 percent contingency, but ultimately, they bottled it.

The news broke that the House voted to impeach Trump in 2019, on the same day that the firm in question had their meeting regarding the final decision on their acceptance of my case. As a result, among the potential media hailstorm it could cause, the law firm got cold feet and decided against it. They choked. They said it had nothing to do with the same-day impeachment vote. Experience has taught me, though, that there are no coincidences.

Once again, I believe God's plan was at work. This decision solidified my own decision to push through to the Durham investigation that had been established. It confirmed to me that I was on my own to try and take action against the Deep State. God had shown me that I could not do much from within; my hands were tied. This moment led me to where I am today.

It reminded me of the core foundation of my strategy to defeat the sinister and invisible "them." The Deep State was able to solidify and dominate because we forgot about ensuring control of our counties, and the counties are the foundation of the vote.

Take control of your county and the country will follow. Do not spend time getting angry about the nation, assert control of the place right between your own two feet. We cannot yet win at the national level.

Not yet.

Who Can You Trust? A Four-Year Pathway to Durham

If my words already are not proof of the fallacy of fighting at the national level, then allow my own struggle to serve as the perfect example. I will share, later in this book, the examples of others who have fought and who have only seen any success at the local level. Allow me now to give you mine.

As you have read, I tried to get my dossier in front of those who needed to see it, from Inspector Generals at both the DOD and the DOJ, up to directors and representatives at the White House. There were a number of people with express interest who helped and who sat outside the lines of accountability, but from those for whom it was their legal duty, I heard nothing.

I decided that I needed a decisive moment, that I myself needed to be faster, more decisive. But most importantly, I wanted to stay on the right side of the law. I still do. This is important to me. There is no point in trying to stand up for the foundations of our nation if I violate the laws that protect it in the process. This was, and is, my moral conviction that supersedes any desire to not be discredited through a legal violation.

I spent all of 2017 running the wickets, sending numerous letters, and receiving no response. Sure, I had people offer to view my evidence digitally, but as I have said, I knew where that would end up, so I pushed for face-to-face meetings, to no avail.

Then, in April 2018, I received a further push, another spur that drove me on at a greater pace. This spur came in the form of an unrelated meeting. This meeting was with someone I trusted, in the offices of an exceptionally powerful and influential former secretary (a known Deep Stater) of the Bush W. administration.

The person I was meeting is a prime example of someone who has no ties to the Deep State but is a victim of the intermingling that occurs in government. As are so many. As was I for a long time before that encounter in the "A" Ring.

As we stopped talking for a coffee break, he casually said to me, "Do you wanna know who is on the other side of that drywall?" His hushed voice told me that it was someone important, and my curiosity was piqued.

"Sure, who is it?"

"General Hayden. It's odd, he's started doing a daily coordination call with Comey, Brennan, and General Clapper," he whispered, "something about information on how to oppose Trump."

Once more, my alarm bells rang, and every hair on my body stood on end. This was potentially explosive, a direct violation of the RICO Act through coordination with Comey, in office as the Director of the FBI, Brennan, now out of office, and General Clapper, also out of office. (And to give credence to my colleague as a victim of intermingling, I have a picture of myself with General Clapper, the Director of National Intelligence at the DNI Christmas party. We have almost all mingled with people who are clearly now the enemy.)

"What!? How do you know?" I almost shouted.

"Shh! These walls are pretty thin. You hear snippets every now and then."

"Who have you spoken to about this?" I asked.

He shrugged. "Nobody, you're the first person I've spoken to about it. What can I do? There's no proof, and these guys hold a way bigger stick than me."

I left it at that. I did not want to pry, and we were burning daylight. I struggled to concentrate for the rest of our meeting, my mind transfixed on the collusion and treason that was happening in the room literally next to me.

This chance encounter once more lit a fire in my belly. I was incensed, things were now out of control, and I vowed once again to be more tenacious, rabid almost, in my pursuit for justice.

This led me to attempt to meet with the Attorney General, William Barr, and the Durham investigation.

Another year passed. I wrote letters to the Attorney General, I spoke to secretaries, but I never got face-to-face with the people who I needed to. I had influential friends trying to help me get the traction to get in front of Barr without raising the kind of noise that would get us noticed by the wrong people. People who could shut us down.

To me, it seemed almost fated that I spent my years serving under the anti-establishment president in my own fight against the establishment.

Then, almost exactly a year later in April 2019, John Durham, the US attorney for Connecticut, was placed in charge of the investigation into the Russian collusion hoax.

It is not uncommon, as part of the additional duties of a US attorney, to be handed an investigation relating to national interest. After all, these are federal employees. Before 2019, Durham was looking into Hillary, investigating her conduct as secretary of state.

By now, I had a dossier containing thirty pages of chronological evidence going back to 2010. What this dossier showed was that this was now full-blown warfare, and I needed to get it into the right hands. I decided that those hands belonged to John Durham.

By hook or by crook, I resolved to get him access to my files, so finally, I got my hands on Durham's phone number after several requests for access were denied. (Remember, I am nothing if not tenacious. Lawful, but tenacious.)

The thing with me is, I did not make it through almost forty years of national security work not being charged or indicted without knowing precisely the legal boundaries to do my operation. This is what makes me the perfect ally in this war.

Now, one piece of advice I can give, and one that has served me well throughout my career is this: be nice to the secretaries. Get to know them. Be kind, make small talk, and take an interest in them. You will be amazed at how far this can carry you and how much influence secretaries actually have.

So, after nearly twenty minutes of conversation, I explained why I needed to speak with Durham, and his secretary asked me to send over a copy of everything I had.

I knew better than to accept this on good faith, so I asked for something in return, some evidence to show that I had submitted evidence to the Durham investigation, and that is what they delivered: a signed letter from John Durham thanking me for my submission, which was updated after the declassification that proved Comey and Brennan knew there was a hoax but chased it still.

This marked the end of a four-year journey since that encounter in the "A" Ring, where I realized there was a uni-party and a Deep State coup.

At the end of this journey, it took me four years to penetrate the bureaucracy. The keyword for this journey is tenacious. There I was, a black belt Judo champion in the affairs of the Swamp, but it took me nearly four years to break through. This is why I know, firsthand, that it is fruitless to try to fight at the national level.

We have to fight at the county level. There, on the ground directly beneath our feet, we can enact real change, and we can gather the momentum we need to strike back, pulling the plug on the Swamp and draining it from below.

Where one journey ended, another began. I joined the fight from outside of Washington, DC, continuing my life of service.

Chapter Six

A Life of Service

A man is not primarily a witness against something. That is only incidental to the fact that he is a witness for something.

Whittaker Chambers

I love my country. I'm an American Patriot—I embrace and love that term no matter how the high priests of Critical Race Theory attempt to shame anyone who uses that moniker. I am a proud patriot wholly, completely, and without reserve. This is the land of opportunity. It is a beautiful country, with some of the most amazing natural landmarks in the world. We have the most amazing people. We are a nation borne out of oppression, unified in our will and desire to overthrow tyranny, and possess a unique collective will to reject it outright—domestically and internationally—which has led to our involvement in dozens of overseas conflicts in support of democracy.

I have given my life in service to this nation and to the principles of democracy and freedom. Power belongs with the people. Governments should operate *for* their people, with the express goal of serving their citizens first. These are values I have lived my life by, and my story is the story of someone who has been to hell and back in service of my country.

Many people go many years not knowing what they stand for or they want from life. *I always knew.* The armed forces of America were in my blood from the very beginning, in my very DNA. As a kid, I would sit on the floor or at the table with my army figures and toy soldiers, devising strategies and counterstrategies.

My father or my older brother would sit opposite me and ask, "What if I took this group here and veered off to the right, to the high ground?" or "Let's imagine it has started raining, how does that change your plan?" They would keep me on my toes, keep me thinking, to the point where I would start planning contingencies without their input, playing against myself. I always had a mind for strategy. It has served me extremely well.

I did not read the books normal kids did. I pored over tomes of influential soldiers and warriors, reading and rereading the stories of various conflicts and their heroes.

World War Two was a particular obsession of mine. Of my inspirations, the story of Audie Murphy has always stood out. I do not remember how I came across his book, *To Hell And Back* (which would go on to become a movie in 1955), but I was enraptured and enchanted by the story of the most decorated soldier of the Second World War and his exploits over two years of continuous combat in North Africa, Italy, France, and Germany that resulted in being awarded the greatest military accolade there is: the Medal of Honor.

There was also *The Green Berets* by Robin Moore written in the early '60s before the Vietnam Syndrome really took over, and *The Longest Day* by Cornelius Ryan, books that truly stand out to me in a library of wartime trivia and knowledge. It was these that inspired me and took my imagination down a path that would lead me to reality.

As far as TV goes, I was drawn to a show called *The FBI*. This was back when we could trust the FBI, back when people in power and positions of authority had a clear moral starting foundation and a known starting point.

The regular theme for me in the things that I watched and read was that of a "righteous cause," the battle of good vs. evil. This mirrored the everyday situations in which I grew up, where news broadcasters warned us daily of the communist threat, and we routinely held drills and received pamphlets concerning what we should do in the not-so-unlikely event of a nuclear attack.

This is something that I do not believe younger generations understand about the environment in which my generation grew up. We lived with the daily threat of total annihilation; white light and a mushroom cloud that could wipe a city off the map. We grew up in a life-or-death struggle against communism, and there were so many nuclear weapons that were held continuously at the ready. This imbues everyone with a healthy level of preparedness and suspicion that lives on throughout your whole life. It makes you question *everything*.

On that note, I remember the constant battle that the government faced to protect us, one that many people opposed, and how it would not be uncommon to see missiles and defense systems in your own neighborhood. I remember the Nikes and Safeguard.

The Nikes were air defense systems that we had around most cities. These were missiles that were right in your neighborhood, and they had nuclear warheads. You could drive home from school and see these missiles with their nuclear warheads.

Safeguard was the original antimissile system—missiles designed to shoot down other missiles. A large controversy erupted around Safeguard that I recall dominating the news for a significant amount of time. The first Safeguard base (and these missiles had nuclear warheads too) was going to be extremely close to downtown Seattle at the now shut down, but very scenic Fort Lawton, and the proposed Safeguard deployment created a massive set of protests in the city, which were extremely divisive between those who wanted the protection this system granted and those who did not want to be at such proximity to nukes. Ultimately, they were not installed.

I remember these protests at Fort Lawton, where hippies protested at an army base that is not there anymore. I witnessed this personally, and I remember siding with the people who wanted to put the missiles in. My attitude was, *Why wouldn't we want to protect ourselves from evil communism?* In hindsight, placing these nuclear missiles in downtown Seattle may have not been the right location, but Seattle—and America—needed the missile defense. It is of great concern that the Continental American city most likely to be vaporized in a nuclear exchange with militant China is Seattle. But then again, with the abject chaos and "woke-ism" the city has descended into, it is not clear that anyone would notice the destruction from a Chinese ballistic missile in Seattle. So, my formative years were spent instilling a drive to protect and serve, and it is a drive that has lived on throughout my life. It is the reason that I wrote this book.

My Witness

To complete the foundation for my belief system, my personal testimony must be given. Without a known starting point in life, there is no such thing as morality or beliefs. A belief can be whatever you want it to be. This is what is going on in America. With Critical Race Theory, the foundation and known starting point are twofold: grievance and narcissism. With that as a starting point, the outcome is simple. The disciple of Critical Race Theory is indoctrinated to hate their country and their fellow citizen. With grievance, there will never be resolution or reconciliation. The teachings are simple. You are oppressed, someone took something from you, and the government will get it back. This is nothing but a nihilistic, never-ending circle of nothingness. It is a perpetual jobs program of a sinister nature.

The ever-present partner to grievance is narcissism, which makes the focus of our interests ourselves. Through narcissism, God is not the center of our beliefs, we are; what I want is what is important.

And the soft science supporting Critical Race Theory (CRT) frees the individual from boundaries where I can justify anything I want or want to be. There are no laws of gravity, physics, or math to prove or disprove the CRT assertions. It is emotion and desire toward the fuzzy end state of Utopia. "I can be whatever I want to be," asserts the scion of CRT. I was born one gender, but I want to be another gender. I am multiple genders. It will never end.

To that, I respond simply: I identify as an endangered sea turtle and the government owes me free oceanfront property and a 10,000-square-foot house. That is my answer, and I'm sticking to it is an appropriate answer to this line of reasoning.

My known starting point is a belief in Jesus Christ. I am a saved believer who will live in eternity in Heaven. There is a Father, Son, and Holy Spirit in one Godhead. Shortly after I began dating my wife, I knew she was the one. I liked her a lot; I loved her. She was pretty, and I was attracted to her. She made it clear, though, that I needed to be saved if this was going to go any further. My wife had led one life before she was saved, and it always fell short, always disappointed. My wife and her two sisters became saved believers in Christ, and it transformed their lives.

Ephesians 4:22–24

22 That ye put off concerning the former conversation the old man, which is corrupt according to the deceitful lusts;

23 And be renewed in the spirit of your mind;

24 And that ye put on the new man, which after God is created in righteousness and true holiness.

This passage is what she shared with me. She set up counseling with her, me, and Pastor Sears and Mrs. Sears. I was led through the Romans Road Plan of Salvation.

1. All have sinned. (Romans 3:10 & Romans 3:23)
2. The penalty for sin is death in hell. (Romans 5:12 & Romans 6:23)
3. Jesus died on the cross to pay the penalty of sin and rose again. (Romans 6:23 & Romans 5:8)
4. Salvation is a free gift that must be accepted. (Romans 10:9–10 & Romans 10:13)

From that moment on, beginning in early 1989, I went forward and never looked back. Of course, I was not perfect and never will be. That is the human condition. A church is full of imperfect people, so join them and feel comfortable. This is my foundation, my testimony, my witness, and my known starting point.

God, Family, Country

I live my life according to three key values: God, Family, and Country. These values define everything I do, and I live purely in service to these three values and my three great loves. I love my God, I love my family, and I love my country.

In the same way that He blessed me with a calling in my early years, God has also given me the gift of endurance and productivity: I wear people out! I'm tenacious, like a dog with a bone, and I never give up, not where justice, faith, my family, and my country are concerned.

In service to my country, what I have found is that, just like in the Old Testament, we have more bad kings than good kings. We always have a leader, a boss, someone who is in charge, and it is more often than not the case that these are mediocre or just plain bad, useless, or ineffective. I have experienced a career limited by being throttled, where I have been held back and governed down instead of being unleashed to achieve my full potential.

They were not all like that, though, I had some good bosses along the way, some inspiring leaders who unleashed me rather than hindered me. One such person was General Stan McChrystal. General McChrystal served his country loyally in his astute leadership of Delta Force. We have all heard of Delta Force (the informal name for our best of the best special operators). We all know their reputation as the elite, the best of the best.

General McChrystal was ultimately betrayed and fired by Obama, despite his amazing contribution to our nation's security and despite spending five continuous years away from his family in service to America because he spoke loosely with *Rolling Stone Magazine.*

He is a great man, and one who saw my potential and unleashed me, naming me as one of the leaders tasked with helping to organize Iraqi regime exiles to overthrow Saddam. I often recall my favorite quip from McChrystal at the Pentagon: "stand up the Joint Staff Over-Reaction Cell."

He was a consummate professional yet knew well the dysfunctional behavior of the beast. I am still concerned, based on some of his own comments, that he may have been part of the orchestrated chaos of the 2020 election to block Trump from a second term.

What I have in abundance is faith. I have absolute faith not just in God, that God put me in certain situations and has guided me down a clear path, but I have faith in our Constitution—that it will ultimately win out in the end.

The truth is, society is devolving. Boundaries are disappearing and eroding, borders seemingly do not exist. Global communication is instant, and societal norms are growing ever abnormal. Society will continue to devolve, but the Constitution is incredible and eternal. It is inevitable, undeniable in its strength and purity, and serves as the perfect tool to protect us as society continues to devolve. The Constitution, the democracy it protects, is the best weapon we have in our arsenal.

But it is not the only weapon; we also have the Bible. The Bible is the only perfect word, the only word that is wholly true and perfect in its reading. The Bible tells us to fight oppression, to live for freedom, and to protect the vulnerable. It tells us to overthrow tyrants and that God will bless those who keep faith in their hearts as they work for the betterment of mankind. Daniel purposed himself to fight in his captivity—that is what we must do in our current captivity.

What this tells us is that we cannot lose because God is with us so long as we keep Him in our hearts. God will give us the steadfast strength that we need to win this fight. God is in control, and this gives me absolute faith that we will be victorious.

Of course, we cannot do this without the strength and love of our families. If the amazing women of Loudoun County have shown us anything, it is that the power of the family is irrefutable.

These moms are motivated by a determined resolve to protect their children, and if we all adopt and live according to that same value, then we can move mountains. The godless Deep State places wealth, power, and influence above all else, forsaking love and faith, and this is what makes them weak. They will fly their white-tailed surveillance aircraft over these meetings in Loudoun County and other places to collect intelligence and intimidate. But it will not work, they will fail, and we will win. They serve only themselves; they only have their own selfish needs and wants to fight for.

We have so much more. We have those whom we love. I have my wife, my son, my daughters, and all of those whom I have the honor to call family, and believe me when I tell you, I would kill for them. I am driven fully by God and display it in an imperfect way, partially through service to my country and partially for the safety and security of those I love. I want to build a better world and a better future for them, and I will stop at nothing to make this happen.

Finally, I am driven by the knowledge that this is the greatest nation on Earth and that the people of the United States of America deserve to live in freedom, free from fear, oppression, and tyranny.

I consider this mission an extension of my career in service to the people of America. It is the people of America who have paid my wages, who are my boss, and to whom I am eternally indebted.

What angers me beyond words is that the American government is owned by the American people, and yet we are denied the transparency to see what is really going on. Those who try to look behind the curtain, to examine and reveal what is really going on, are branded as conspiracy theorists. They are ridiculed and defamed, their legitimacy robbed from them before they are thrown on the pile.

Government should exist to serve the needs of the people, not the needs of the few. There should be no private agendas, backroom deals, and corporate power struggles.

How dare people of wealth, status, and power put down American citizens! Sorry to be putting the pieces together, but these are the same people who just headed up the FDA and then gracefully pivoted over to run Pfizer… it does not take a genius to put these pieces together, and I am not an idiot or a conspiracy theorist.

The American people are being criminalized for critical thinking. They are being censored, blocked, removed from social media platforms, and belittled by the media, their struggles and their battles trivialized.

As a senior civil servant, I always took my oath of office with the gravest sincerity. This oath meant, and very much still means, everything to me. As such, and as I have already alluded to, I would regularly receive vast numbers of calls in my office inside the Pentagon from average Americans. I made it my mission to give these folks at least fifteen minutes, where they could communicate and have a direct line into the government that they paid for. I wanted to give people the ability to have their questions answered; they deserved that at least.If somebody wanted to try and achieve a government contract, as was often the basis of these calls, I would try and give them the basic information that they needed—nothing classified or privileged—I would just explain the process as much as possible. After all, that person was paying my salary, as I would often tell my bosses or colleagues who said, "Hang up on that person, they're just crazy." There is too much of that attitude across government.

My goal was, is, and always has been, to serve God, my family, and my country. If we all adopt these values, then we cannot lose.

Breaching the Berm

My years in the military were the proudest of my life. The pinnacle of that pride came in the breaching of the Iraqi Border Berm at the beginning of the First Gulf War (we called it Desert Shield/Desert Storm at that time) when I saw the vast, well-trained, well-resourced American military lead an international coalition to demolish the Iraqi military in the blistering sands of the Middle East.

What is not well understood or appreciated is that the First Gulf War still sits front and center in the thinking of the Chinese and Russians. They hold our performance in the First Gulf War as the Gold Standard of warfare. It put the fear of God into them—at least in our high art form of synchronized statecraft.

The Iraqi Berm was, quite literally, the wall built of sand between Saudi Arabia and Iraq going back ten years, but hastily improved during the First Gulf War. The Iraqis were "Soviet" in their doctrine and equipment, and this was a Stalingrad Berm and Tank Ditch on a grand scale. When Saddam decided in 1990 that Kuwait was a part of Iraq and invaded in a Soviet textbook "bigger country invading a smaller, weaker country" scenario (history is littered with these), Iraqi forces rolled right through all obstacles and defensive efforts, occupying large parts of Kuwait. In response, Uncle Sam decided that enough was enough and resolved to send in the cavalry and defend the freedom of the people of Kuwait, maintaining stability in the region.

At the time I was leading the army's first modern drone unit, but I was desperate not to miss this, so I approached our brigade commander in his office and stood at attention.

"What can I do for you, Mills?" he said, barely lifting his head from his desk.

"Sir, I've been here for a couple of years. I don't want to miss this, I want to go directly to the front in Kuwait and Saudi Arabia to be part of Desert Shield."

He looked up at me and sat back in his chair.

"You and a thousand others, so why you? Why should you go?" he asked me.

"Sir, I have done everything that has been asked of me and more. I have shown my determination and skill. I'm in the zone for rotation, I can't miss this. I'm ready to go," I replied, pleading my case.

He looked me up and down for a minute, the silence agonizing. I met his gaze, and he simply said, "I'll be back with you shortly, dismissed."

That, I assumed, was that. Perhaps I had been too audacious in going directly to the brigade commander, and I sheepishly left the room, assuming that this opportunity would just pass me by.

But it did not. My audacity had worked.

Later that night, as I sat regretting my actions, I received a call that would send me to the Gulf.

"First Lieutenant Mills, pack your bags, and in the morning, report to Third Armored Cavalry Regiment, currently loading out at Fort Bliss, Texas."

As I put down the receiver, I sat for a moment in stunned silence. It had worked! A whole life of preparation had led me here, about to fly to the Middle East, and I was going with the Third Armored Cavalry Regiment. This seemed prophetic to me. The "Brave Rifles" was a unit I had read so much about throughout my youth, a unit that dated all the way back to the Mexican-American War of 1846 when they famously stormed Chapultepec Castle in Mexico City, and thus, the legend of the "Brave Rifles" was born.

Just a few days later, we were en route from Fort Bliss to Saudi Arabia. The first thing I remember about Saudi Arabia is the heat. As soon as the plane doors opened, a gust of warm air filled the hold, like opening an oven, only that oven was going to be our battlefield.

This was a challenge to adjust to, especially when carrying sixty pounds of gear on your back. The next was the light. The sun was blinding, and you could not look down for relief because the light reflected off the sand. The first days were spent adjusting to this alien atmosphere, a climate unlike anything I had experienced before. I thought I knew heat from Texas. I was wrong.

We did not have too much time to adapt, though. The Brave Rifles moved shortly from the port of Jubail in Saudi Arabia along the Tap Line road—the historical road supporting oil drilling.

First we moved to assembly areas and training areas and then in a great sweep to the left to assume the right flank of the 18th Airborne Corps. Actions along the border began almost immediately.

On February 24, 1991, the full might of the US military gathered and advanced over the Berm, and I saw it in all of its glory. It was the vision of a lifetime, the might of the US Army as it poured into Iraq, It was the biggest advance by American and Allied forces since World War Two. There were American forces as far as the eye could see, and I could see it all. I was part of a small party overlooking our immediate front elements as they breached the Iraqi Berm.

For the next month, we rolled through the desert engaging in ground combat action and consolidation after the collapse and defeat of the Iraqi forces. My role in this was in our intelligence vehicle, or in the "jump" TOC (Tactical Operations Center), as the mini-command and intelligence cell with the unit commander in his Bradley Scout Vehicle. There were no fancy heads-up displays or drone maps; I relied on a map and three radios: one in my right ear, a different one in my left ear, and a third one close by.

In among the booming and banging of gunfire and artillery shelling, I ran the map board and relayed intelligence and information to the units around us. And the desert is not as smooth as glass, it is littered with pits and ravines, so I was managing the coordination of our frontline units while being thrown around the stiflingly hot cabin of an armored vehicle and bracing for a possible rollover of the Bradley.

Our success was breathtaking. As we breached, and in the subsequent campaign, we took remarkably few casualties. In fact, our first immediate casualties were our squadron commander and command sergeant major, who both suffered from heart attacks before and during the initial deployment. As I said, this was a punishing environment, and the stress on the body was incredible.

God certainly blessed our operation. We swarmed on top of our enemy with breathtaking speed, so fast in fact that often we came upon them by surprise, the enemy completely unaware of our advance. We were on them so fast that almost everybody surrendered. We surprised everybody, even ourselves to an extent. The American Eagle was in full flight, and nobody could resist us.

The M-1 Abrams tank is also known as "Whispering Death." It is astonishingly quiet. Often the only way you know one is coming is by the odd, buttery smell that comes from the exhaust until it is right on top of you. This smell comes from the gas turbine engine, which gives it its immense speed and power. I became all too familiar with this smell. Desert nights can be incredibly cold, and to warm oneself, you would often walk behind the exhaust of the M1 at night. We advanced at night because it hid any sand clouds that billowed behind us and our night vision equipment gave us a great advantage over the Iraqis, who were limited by the equipment left over from the Soviets.

To this extent, I recall, in the early days of the invasion, that we got out of our tanks after overrunning an objective and inspected the equipment that the Iraqis had left behind. We found that it was mostly Russian and Chinese equipment, including Russian T-72s. What struck us was that most of these vehicles had significant damage from our aircraft or our direct fire weapons. I recalled seeing this equipment on TV from broadcasted Red Square parades where it all looked very impressive and scary. I can tell you that they did not look as impressive when they were destroyed in the desert.

I also remember the first Iraqi soldier that we captured and that I had to handle. It was odd. This man was just walking along the desert, with no civilization for miles on either side. He had no weapons, no bag of equipment, just a large briefcase full of cash. We had no idea why. I had an Arab-speaking US soldier detailed to the intelligence section, and the Iraqi appeared to be an officer abandoning his unit. The Iraqi Dinar was essentially worthless, so this heavily-laden briefcase was, in real terms, worth mere pennies.

Early March 1991 was a notorious period of indecision where we were told to halt and not to advance any further other than to establish security zones in front of our front line. This decision led to intense debate among the staff group, with a clear split between those in favor of advancing and those in favor of halting.

My position was clear: I felt, and still do to this day, that we needed to advance all the way to Baghdad, using this shock and awe momentum to take us all the way to Saddam's doorstep. I felt that if we did not, we would be back again. And what do you know, but a little over ten years later, we were back, and I was back in Baghdad.

As I look back now, I wonder to what extent external influences, and by that, I mean conflicting interests within the government, contributed to this decision. It certainly benefited many people acting within the US government to keep Saddam in place.

In hindsight, the First Gulf War represented the beginning of the Forever War mindset, one that has plagued the American national security apparatus to the present day. And for the Deep State, conflict is good. Conflict divides people, and division prevents people from unifying. Protests and anger have followed every interventional conflict throughout the twentieth and twenty-first centuries and have pitted people directly against their neighbors, which plays directly into the hands of the Deep State. I'm all in support of a powerful military—but only under an America First mindset. Its purpose is to deter opponents and conflict and only decisively engage when necessary, not create a circular conveyor belt of enduring conflict. Let us not forget as well that the plutarchy that sits at the helm of the Deep State possesses complex and deep ties to the global military-industrial complex, for whom war represents a direct revenue stream.

Psyops in Bosnia

I learned a lot about peacemaking among multiple parties in complex environments in Bosnia. Few times in history are things as simple as the First Gulf War. We are good, they are bad; we line up in a grand line and run over them. This was the basic operational overview of the First Gulf War. Bosnia was much more emblematic of complex environments with multiple combatants. In many ways, it is a closer model to the current conflict in American society.

To see the power of division truly at work, I need to think no further than 1997.

Bosnia was, at the time of the Yugoslavian civil war, a true hellscape; a myriad of deserted towns as empty as the shells of buildings that remained, where every day you played hopscotch over minefields. As Yugoslavia collapsed, awakening from the stupor of decades of communism and the withdrawal symptoms brought about by the loss of Russian support, every nationality and faction awoke to stake their claim on their homeland. People of wealth, status, and power seized upon ethnicity and religion to divide the population and the tools to retain their wealth, status, and power. Unfortunately, the population obliged.

You had the Bosnians, the Croats, Kosovans, Albanians, Montenegrins, Macedonians, and Slovenians, all of whom had the same objective but vastly different means of achieving it. The objective was to achieve their independence and the autonomy of the region and to overturn and reject the rule of the Serbs, who were universally rejected as they were considered Russian. It was the Serbs who picked up the mantle of communism and attempted to carry it forward, and they did so through brutal oppression and ethnic cleansing. These are the familiar tactics of those attempting to instill a supposedly utopian way of living.

At this time, Russia was financially and economically broken, picking up the pieces of the shattered union. It was the view of Clinton's Secretary of State, Madeleine Albright, that we should kick Russia further in the teeth by taking any semblance of control of the Balkans away from the Russian government in what was a glowing example of the Forever War mentality. And Putin remembers this.

Although the Russians were on the ground partners in the stabilization force implementing the Dayton Peace Accords, Albright and the State Department deemed the Serbians the bad side; hence the Russians were bad because of their allegiance to their Slavic brothers and sisters. There was a brief window in the '90s where reconciliation with the Russians was possible. Albright made sure that would not happen.

This Forever War mentality has made a very small number of people incredibly wealthy. The military-industrial complex is the playground of those who seek to hold power behind the scenes, and they use it to keep nations divided, fighting, and using their equipment and weapons to do so. And it was not just weapons systems that filled their coffers but the private contract services too. Halliburton KBR is a great example of this. When the conflict began, our bases of operations were temporary, mobile. When the life support contract with Halliburton KBR was signed, these temporary structures and camps, situated right in the middle of warzones, were suddenly comfortable. Disarmingly so.

Halliburton made these temporary camps more permanent, and the more permanent the infrastructure, the easier it was for the military to slip into the malaise of focusing not on a strategic end state but more on the routine of filling and executing the deployment cycle.

In other words, the generals and admirals are more focused on process than end state. I worked as a staff officer under three generals: General Meigs, General Casey, and General Abizaid, who were to become the leading army general officers in Operation Iraqi Freedom, and I would work with them later on in the Joint Staff (Meigs was retired by OIF but also assumed a critical role in retirement.)

KBR were everywhere. They did your laundry, provided food—home comforts too—and they erected fences around base camps. They made the uncomfortable a lot more comfortable, making war bearable and, therefore, perpetual. And they were a driving factor with a vested interest in perpetuating the Forever War. It was in their interests, and those of their benefactors, to continue the war and keep us fighting. So they made it easier for us.

What is not often spoken about is the Islamic element of the war in Yugoslavia. Islamic expansion did as much to perpetuate the Forever War as those elements within our own government(s) and the military-industrial complex, to the point where, looking back, the connection between them seems clear. Of course, at the time, where the rhetoric was far different and you were actively fighting them, that was much harder to see, and I believed wholeheartedly in the honest intentions of all those involved in establishing and enforcing peace in Yugoslavia.

There were many odd, slightly surprising connections to Islam. They existed within the Bosnian populations, which I suppose makes a little sense given the former occupation by the Islamic Ottoman Empire. Yet Tito had done a pretty thorough job of repressing religious expression, so it was surprising to see Islamic themes and identities arising within the Bosnian population.

A significant element of this was the Mujahideen, or the "Mujis" as we referred to them. The same Mujahideen that was run by Osama Bin Laden, you know the one, the one that committed the most heinous act of terrorism the globe has ever seen and that we, in our avarice, funded to oppose the USSR in Afghanistan. Little did the planners and implementers of Operation Cyclone[11] realize that their actions were establishing the framework for perpetual conflict.

My job in Bosnia was to enable the implementation of the Dayton Peace Accords with a steady drumbeat of psyops messages aimed at the target audiences of the various factions operating across Bosnia. We created a steady stream of information broadcasts in radio and television form, and I went through many linguists until a core of three trusted translators emerged.

Translation and presentation in media of broadcasts are difficult and not for everyone. It could be quite stressful for the contract linguists. We seemed to develop an efficient process that could deliver products in a smaller and smaller period of time. Quickness of production and delivery

---

11.https://warontherocks.com/2019/02/afghanistan-remembering-the-long-long-war-we-would-rather-forget/

was essential when competing with Bosnian, Serb, Croat, and Muslim media that could conduct broadcasts almost immediately, unhindered by any sense of standards of conduct, quality, or accuracy. My core team consisted of a Bosnian (with Muslim heritage), a Serb, and a Croat. We put out almost eight hundred segments during my tour.

I was not clear on our effectiveness until a Special Forces Operational Detachment (known as "ODAs," Operational Detachment Alphas, your classic Special Forces "A" Team) senior noncommissioned officer and his colleague tracked me down and showed me his "man on the street" interviews, where they were documenting and quantifying who was listening to what and their thoughts on the topic. This was brilliant and provided the feedback necessary to "tune" our psyops. Although psyops sounds sinister and malign, the American military version (when properly conducted by the Special Operations Community) is quite simple: tell the truth at all times.

The data rendered by the Special Forces Team was essential information (maybe intelligence) to help develop the human terrain map—the key center of gravity in many multiparty civil war situations. I asked him to share this, and I would accept all the reports. So multiple Special ODAs started replicating this model and providing these reports. The bottom line was simple: the Bosnians liked us, the Serbs did not like us, and the Croats were perhaps a bit on the fence. Regardless, all listened and watched us. We were continually in the top three of the fifteen to twenty media options available.

Not bad, not bad at all.

Back to the additional duty of Monitoring the Mujis, this fell into the job jar of the Special Operations Community (which psyops was part of). In truth, at the time I did not really understand why they were there. They proved elusive, using the shells of bombed buildings, abandoned sewers, and tunnel systems to keep their actions hidden. For them, the war represented an opportunity to maintain the Forever Conflict of expanding Islam into the West, though I did not completely understand this at the time. I had not yet connected the dots or understood the strategic significance of their presence among the myriad of combatants.It was during this psyops (a noncombative operation aimed at influencing a target population's state of mind) that I saw firsthand how they were operating. You see, to understand how to undermine an enemy, you first have to understand how they work, what their motivations are, and what their agenda is.

Reconnaissance had shown that the Islamists were operating out of a set of once-deserted ruins. Camps and enclaves had appeared in many deserted settlements, and they often had spending money to hand out to help curry favor and interest from the impoverished Bosnians. Most had little if any interest or allegiance to Islam, but a 40–60 Deutschmarks-a-month stipend in return for the women of the house wearing Islamic headgear and going to the mosque on Fridays was appealing to many.

So, when we would send expert personnel to observe and report on them, the Mujis would sense our presence and seek to escape and evade this monitoring. This was a tactic that they used expertly in the caves of Western Afghanistan and Eastern Pakistan later in the war against the Taliban and previously against the Soviets: keep moving, hiding, make the enemy chase them, and then ambush them, before retreating back into the caves.

The first thing on your mind as you entered an empty town like this, regardless of whether it had been swept, are Improvised Explosive Devices (IEDs) and mines hidden among the scree, rubble, and craters between the shattered, collapsed, and hollowed-out buildings. I remember it well as we made our way down the "safe routes" closely watching every step and those of the men walking in front of me. We did not want to be the first casualties of a missed mine.

Even on my own base camp, there were marked paths to walk, and I remember watching a large antitank mine emerge over time from the Bosnian muddy muck just a couple of feet off the marked "safe" pathway to the gym until the EOD element safely detonated it.

The Islamist enclaves and "evangelism" was confusing—but much of the multi-faction conflict was confusing.

This was a surprise to us. The Mujahideen, or the El Mudzahid, had originally fought on the side of the Bosnian rebels when they first arrived in 1992. The new goal, so this intel told us, was to destabilize the local Bosnian population and drum up support for the Islamic cause, which would only serve to perpetuate the conflict and keep neighborhoods and communities fighting. They were engaging in a psyops of their own, only theirs involved guns and murder.

This was one of the first moments in which I privately asked critical questions about the war in which I was fighting. Not only of its combatants but of our role in it. On reflection, I know the answers to many of these questions, and I knew them then but denied them to myself.

What I was watching, and was a part of, was a clear parallel between modern-day conflicts and wars that took place decades ago. I was watching the onset of a conflict that would never end, that would simply shift location and combatants, but was intrinsically linked.

In Bosnia, people of wealth, status, and power were working to get the population to fight one another, and despite having the same goals and mutual opposition, the multitude of factions that were operating throughout the former Yugoslavia was fighting not just their mutual enemy but each other.

And throughout this, Muslim extremists were gathering power.

Bosnia was emblematic of complex civil unrest, which is exactly what we are facing right now in our Constitutional-based society. It is being stoked by the Deep State, and we need to have a steel resolve to endure and regain the initiative and the centers of power that have corrupted the application of our Constitution. The centers of power for governance and elections in America are based on the foundation of the county.

Chapter Seven

The Day the World Changed

A great people has been moved to defend a great nation. Terrorist attacks can shake the foundations of our biggest buildings, but they cannot touch the foundation of America. These acts shatter steel, but they cannot dent the steel of American resolve.

George W. Bush, September 11, 2001

On the day the world changed, I was in San Antonio on a government trip. When working in government, you often have to take the opportunities for some time away whenever you can. We were homeschooling, and it made sense to take my ten-year-old son with me as "some time away." We figured he could stay in the room during the day and do his school assignments while I was at the meeting.

September 11 was a warm day as the last vestiges of summer were beginning to give way to fall. I was in my hotel room when I heard the news. In fact, I was standing in front of the mirror, shaving before the meeting that morning, which was to be held right down the hall from our hotel room.

As I was cleaning up, my ears caught a concerned voice from my son.

"Dad, come to the TV! Something is happening!" The tone of his voice was quite different from his normal morning tone. He had awoken in a good mood, so this sudden change concerned me. It was clear that he had recognized something highly unusual was going on. At that time, Fox was a trusted news source, and my morning routine was to have *Fox and Friends* on in the morning. Steve Doocy and Brian Kilmeade were my television "friends" whom I felt a close kinship with.

It was a few minutes before 9:03 a.m. Eastern Standard Time, 8:03 a.m. Central Standard Time. I emerged just in time to see Brian Kilmeade and Steve Doocy narrating as the second plane slammed into the towers. Brian, Steve, my son, and I were all confused.

Was this a replay of the aircraft hitting the North Tower? I was numb with shock, paralyzed by the instant knowledge that the world had changed forever.

I could scarcely make a sound beyond "… oh my…" as questions raced through my head: *How has this happened? Who did this? How many people have been killed? What are we going to do about this?* The thoughts raced faster than I could process them. I was awakened from my stupor by the sound of my Palm Pilot alarm reminding me about the meeting I was scheduled to attend, so after briefly comforting my son and promising a swift return, I pulled on my jacket and made my way down the hall to the large conference room.

After a few steps, I joined my colleagues at the start of the planning meeting in the hotel conference room, each as shocked as I. Many had relatives in New York and Washington, DC, and this was before the time of smartphones, so none of us had any means of checking updates other than legacy flip phones. And although I had a special access card that was supposed to give me priority access on the phone lines during national emergencies, surprise surprise, that system was overwhelmed.

My parents were on a once-in-a-lifetime trip to Australia, and my wife was visiting her parents in Arizona. The master of ceremonies tried to begin the large meeting but prefaced it with a number of references, prayers, and uncertainty as to what exactly was going on. The anxiety in the conference room was palpable, unbearable, and as the meeting started, nobody was able to pay attention, and the room was filled with the din of whispered conversations as we all tried to squeeze whatever information we could out of each other.

Before long, the inevitable happened, the meeting organizers announced the meeting was canceled, and the orders were clear.

Return to Your Home Station

What followed was chaos as each of us bundled to the door, made calls, frantically sent messages, and hurtled off toward our rooms.

I ran down the hall to our fortuitously close room. "Son, we need to pack the bags as fast as possible. Don't worry about it being neat, we need to get back to DC." He was a trooper as he quickly cleared the room, bundled our belongings into suitcases, and rushed back to our car. I worked with two coworkers at the meeting who lived relatively close to me to hastily obtain a rental car. I was astonished at the speed with which we were able to get to the airport to pick up the car. And we had to be quick.

The line formed quickly behind us as word spread like fire that all flights were canceled.

Coincidentally, I never mentioned the purpose of the large government assembly in San Antonio: next generation air traffic control systems to greatly advance safety and efficiency of the National Airspace System (NAS). One thing that needed to be added to this NAS imperative: Security from asymmetric and unforeseen threats such as groups dedicated to the destruction of the United States.

As we set off, my son asked over the news reports on the radio, as he tried to make sense out of things, "Things are never going to be the same again, are they, Dad?"

I sighed. "I don't know, son. I'll know more when we get to Washington. Whatever happens, we will look after each other. We will be okay," I reassured him. It was all I could do.

The trip across the country was one I shall never forget. There was constant news, just news bulletin after news bulletin; reports of death, destruction, and tales of unimaginable bravery as rescue services and civilians banded together to pull survivors from the wreckage and comfort the families of those who had fallen. The constant stream of news was occasionally broken up by patriotic music. Remember, this was before pervasive smart phones, broadband cellphones, and the internet. The world was still seen through AM/FM radio when on the move.

Never before had I seen the country so united. It was so incredibly moving to see flags adorning houses, cars, billboards… They were everywhere. In the face of this atrocity, the nation pulled together in the greatest show of national unity I believe any of us had ever witnessed.

We drove for two days, stopping only for comfort breaks and to sleep in Montgomery, Alabama, when we were all exhausted. I say sleep—I got little. I was glued to the news, mining and sifting for any and all information I could get. My son, however, slept well. I have always been astonished at the ability of kids to manage a crisis. They have an amazing resilience I think we could all learn from.

Speculation was rife, and it was not long before Osama Bin Laden and Al-Qaeda took credit, and new themes that would dominate the lexicon of international relations for the next twenty years began to emerge: Islamic terrorism, conspiracy theories, Middle Eastern Geopolitics, Jihad… the list goes on.

The drive home from Texas to DC gave me plenty of time to reflect as my son and I sat, mostly in silence, across from each other. On the one hand, I knew we would be engaged in a period of conflict for an extremely long time. Fighting a war against a dedicated extremist group is a battle of steel wills and resolve—it is a war of survival of ideologies—a test to see who wanted to win most. We learned this only too well during the Cold War. I did not quite understand yet that the Forever War band would have a field day with this conflict.

On the other hand, the show of unity from across the United States of America, and from the international community in general, was astounding. Everybody banded together, sharing their grief, their strength, and their resolve to fight this evil that now threatened American sovereignty. Shortly after I returned home, I received an email from two of my star linguists who were hopeful that myself and my immediate family were safe, but they also urged restraint and discouraged more violence. I respected them deeply and knew they had personally seen and experienced savage butchery in the Bosnian Civil War. I cannot remember whether this email was before or after President George W. Bush's immortal words:

"I can hear you! I can hear you! The rest of the world hears you, and the people who knocked these buildings down will hear all of us soon."

But my words in the email were very clear and similar; this was the beginning of a worldwide war, and America would unleash a ferocious and righteous global pursuit the likes of which the world had never before seen. There was much truth to my thoughts and feelings. At the same time, though, there was much truth to the viewpoints of my former linguists also. One of them was a nonpracticing Muslim and felt great concern over all Muslims being targeted. I was in many ways filled with righteous anger—we will chase these terrorists to the gates of hell—but also wanted to be sure we conducted this worldwide war in a manner that simultaneously was ferocious yet respectful, possibly impossible or at least "unobtanium." It is exceedingly hard to maintain this kind of aspirational imperative in war, which as I know now devolved into the "Forever War" model. No one profits from Forever Wars other than the Deep Staters.

America United

I often reflect on the stark contrast between the American unity that was on show on the drive home after 9/11 and in the immediate days that followed and the atrocity of 2020, where American sovereignty had once again been threatened, this time through an election system that was clearly vulnerable and a growing number of Americans did not trust it.

The Carter Center for Democracy identifies that one of the key indicators of questionable elections is when high numbers of the population, bleeding over into a plurality, assert that there are serious issues with the conduct or outcome of an election. Although there have been attempts to suppress the discussion of any concerns on the election, the public sense and perception continues to grow.

I know some news organizations are under legal assault, but this does not mean people and groups should be silenced. Groups and organizations can defend themselves from lawfare and still be "fair and balanced," as one news organization used to assert and the reason they built such a following until recently.

In 2001, the people establishing the narratives were bringing society together, creating unity and strength around the liberty, freedom, and strength that we hold so very dear. This fervor drummed up the support necessary to begin the War on Terror, which led to the military insertions into Afghanistan, which has been squandered with the humiliating debacle of one of the most poorly conducted evacuations in American military history. President Biden bears personal responsibility for the deaths of the poorly led, planned, and conducted evacuation from Afghanistan and the worldwide descent into chaos with the feckless, America-last assertions of national interest.

In 2001, American patriotism reached a fever pitch, and regardless of political allegiance or affiliation, there was a general sense that together we were stronger and that together we would fight the evil that threatened our nation. Sure, there were disagreements on the means (these disagreements and divisions were magnified in the halls of power), but there was little disagreement on the final objectives: protect the nation, defend the weak, and sow the seeds of democracy.

That was until a Tuesday night, October 29, 2002, when a Memorial Service for Minnesota Senator Paul Wellstone turned into a political riot against all who opposed the rise of Big Government. I remember watching this frenzy of angry diatribes, and thus the period of national solidarity was essentially over. I watched as those with the craven focus of societal control reemerged from the shadows.

The War on Terror did continue, and our national security apparatus were deployed in full force against our enemies, used to actively protect our citizens and defend the liberties of those for whom they were stripped away. The ambition, on the face of it, was noble, and I was at the forefront of planning and implementing a number of these lines of effort. Little did I realize that later they would be turned about and used against the American people en masse.

Leaving the chaos of DC, I was tasked with joining the J5 on Central Command Staff, based out of McDill Air Force Base in Tampa, Florida. The mission: planning the campaign in Afghanistan.

The Department of Defense is replete with plans. Plans for seemingly everything. We were tasked with answering the "how," the "end state," and the "what if" questions that arose from this developing worldwide conflict with the immediate focus on Afghanistan, the center of gravity for Al-Qaeda training, organizing, and equipping. The DOD has lots of plans, but not plans for everything, and we were tasked with bridging this gap—"lofting out" plans of different maturity levels for a variety of contingencies. But the goal, first and foremost, was pursuing the enemy into the gates of hell and destroying them.

In 2001, in the aftermath of the single greatest attack on American sovereign territory, all eyes and minds were geared toward national security and the protection of the Union.

America Divided

Oh, how this differs from America since 2020, where the people establishing the narratives are driving American citizens against each other. In 2001, all eyes were geared toward the defense of America and its allies, from its armed forces to its media apparatus.

However, as we know, to our enemy (the Deep State forces) such unity of the American people is bad in the long-term. It is useful to shepherd the flock in the short-term, but when the flock begins to change direction, the invisible *They* need something to halt that momentum, and nothing works better than scattering the flock, sowing discord and division among the masses.

Now, those institutions that are supposed to be protecting Americans are being used against us. The shameful misuse of our national security apparatus serves to attack Americans when:

1. You are not a threat.

2. The only insurrection that happened was on November 3, 2020, when the democracy of our nation was undermined, and some parts of the nation had no problem with this.

Over twenty years later, the same group of those with wealth, status, and power are driving the American people against each other through restrictions and mandates not based on science and fact but on fear to keep Americans under their control, to get Americans to hate each other and to hate their country.

The greatest attack on American soil was carried out by a group of Islamic terrorists with a disturbing number of links to the Deep State. It was perpetrated by an enemy that we had been actively fighting since the end of the Cold War, and an enemy largely of our own creation, one that we empowered to fight what was a greater enemy. Yet the Soviets never managed anything quite like that.

Did we, in many ways, essentially create the foundations of Al-Qaeda? Yes. We armed the opposition in Afghanistan to grind the Soviets into nothingness. Of that, there is absolutely no question. We gave them arms, plenty of ammunition, and we trained them to use both conventional and unconventional tactics, transforming them into an effective fighting force, armed with tools of subversion and subterfuge, many of which I witnessed being used in Bosnia in the next phase of the war waged by Islam against the West.

And then the Soviets left. The Islamists achieved their objective, albeit with our help. The thing is, those same people did not much like us either. For them, we were a means to an end, but we represented everything that they hated: equality, freedom, and democracy. The only thing that bound us was a mutually disagreeable opponent, and when that opponent was beaten, we became the new enemy.

From the Mujahideen arose Al-Qaeda, led by Osama Bin Laden, and in many ways, we equipped, armed, and financed the foundations from which this group arose. Unfortunately, this is one of the unintended consequences of getting involved in these situations. I do not believe that we deliberately created this enemy, but what we do know is that it is a risk of intervention. It is why we think long and hard about our involvement in these situations. There are many different potential consequences that we cannot anticipate. And let me be clear, we may well have contributed to the horrendous events of 9/11, but I do not believe for one minute that we instigated them—that we attacked ourselves—as the conspiracy theorists would have you believe.

I have gone through the physics of the situation. There is absolutely no question that those buildings were taken out by those roughly 300,000-pound aircraft flying at several hundred miles an hour. The focused shearing force of this mass on a large vertical mass is decisive. There is no alternative that offers sufficient evidence to the contrary.

What allowed this to happen was the wall of separation between intelligence and law enforcement that profligated and grew during the Clinton years. This wall of separation helped to create the environment where we, in essence, lost track of Osama Bin Laden's training activities. We were blinded because of poor policy decisions.

And now we live in a situation that is the polar opposite, where the union of law enforcement and intelligence is used as a tool of oppression instead of one of liberation. Today, these two linchpins of our national security have fused together, to the point where they are indistinguishable, creating a weapon that is being actively used against the American citizen.

Herein exists a dichotomy. This wall of separation actually serves a purpose. I mean, if we had that wall today, would we have had the internal spying and leaking that plagued President Trump? Would we have the spying on American citizens that plagues us all daily? Maybe, just maybe, we would not have had the election coup of 2020.

Who knows? No mere mortal can see around so many corners and predict the future. But what we do know is that, since 9/11, the national sense of unity that drew us all together is gone, deliberately eroded, and corroded by the tools that should be promoting its growth. And these tools are now actively sowing discord and division to prevent a collective awakening that has the power and potential to bring power back to we, the people.

The true legacy of 9/11 is that the Deep State recognized the power that we hold when we move as one and doubled down on their efforts to divide us, bringing us to where we are now. I believe that recognizing this—that we are being deliberately pulled apart—has the potential to bring us back together, uniting us against the common enemy, the one that looks to enslave us all.

Part Three

Chapter Eight

The Four Corners of Deceit

"The four corners of deceit: government, academia, science and media. Those institutions are now corrupt and exist by virtue of deceit. That's how they promulgate themselves; it is how they prosper."

Rush Limbaugh

In order to defeat the enemy you have to first understand it. Over the years, I had become a highly trained national security professional in understanding the enemy and developing plans to identify and defeat these threats to America. In the Cold War, it was the Soviets. In the Peace Dividend, it was warring factions in civil wars, and in the War on Terror, it was Islamic Extremists. Finally, starting in 2010, it was China.

I had been called in twice to be informed that I (and a small group of others) were in the crosshairs of the Chinese, alongside ISIS. I later remarked to a senior FBI official that I was not sure if it was my role in the Combined Federal Campaign (the annual campaign inside the federal government to raise funds for nonprofit groups) or some other mundane administrative task that triggered their interest, but regardless, let's give them something to talk about and spin them into the ceiling. He liked that answer a lot.

But around 2010, I began to realize it was not only China and ISIS threatening America, it was also elements within our own government and society. Until I heard Donald J. Trump use the term Deep State or the Swamp, I called it the Four Corners of Deceit in America.

One important matter is the oath of office that military members and also civil servants take before assuming office. The sworn oath states:

"I ___, do solemnly swear (or affirm) that I will support and defend the Constitution of the United States against all enemies, foreign and domestic; that I will bear true faith and allegiance to the same; that I take this obligation freely, without any mental reservation or purpose of evasion; and that I will well and faithfully discharge the duties of the office on which I am about to enter. So help me God. (Title 5 US Code 3331, an individual, except the President, elected or appointed to an office of honor or profit in the civil service or uniformed services)."

I take this oath incredibly seriously. I began to realize what this means as I waded further through the muck, and I have come to the realization that many do not or have wildly elastic interpretations of what this means.

The Deep State, for all its machinations, scheming, and controversies is remarkably easy to summarize and describe. The goal is simple: domination and control. To do this, they occupy the Four Corners of society that have created and granted the Deep State the greatest amount of control, influence, and sway. These are:

1. Big Government
2. Big Academia
3. Big Tech
4. Big Finance

These Four Corners penetrate and permeate every facet of our lives, giving those that seek control an inordinate amount of power, a power that is invisible to the naked eye and yet profoundly obvious and all-encompassing. And they have poisoned all four of them with deceit.

They enact control on the government, our education structures and information dissemination, our technological advancements and information gathering, and on our financial systems, allowing them to exert their influence on everything that makes society tick.

The only thing they do not (yet) control is the people. Sure, they control large swathes of society, but a rough approximation is that they control roughly 20 percent of the population—those who are actively part of these four groupings. That leaves 80 percent of the population. In my role as a seasoned and skilled National Security Jedi, the conclusion is obvious. We are the majority.

Well, if we are the majority, we need to start acting like it.

An ever-growing number of people are beginning to wake up and see this subversion, resulting in an immense ground swell of antiestablishment sentiment. The free will that we exude is contagious and proves that for all of their attempts at domination, they are doomed to fail. As long as we have free will, we have the power to fight, reject, and overthrow this tyranny and oppression.

So, let us dive into who they are in some detail, lifting the lid on their control structures so that we have a true picture of how to fight back and what the battlefields are.

Big Government

This first Corner comes, I am sure, as no surprise. I have already alluded to and spoken of the influence that the Deep State holds within the corridors of power in every facet of our governing structures. Not until the very end of my career did I realize I was in one of the Four Corners of Deceit.

The Deep State holds influence at every level of our government, starting right at the top. Their influence in the White House waned somewhat during the Trump years. You see, Trump rejected them. All of our presidents knew of the existence of the Deep State. For many of them, it was their way into power—making a deal with the proverbial devil.

Trump was not the first to reject them, but he was certainly the loudest and the most defiant, sparking an antiestablishment populism that threatened the Deep State's power in the upper echelons of government.

Now that Trump is out and Ice Cream Joe is in, that control has come back in full swing and is once again exercising a heavy hand over policy decisions. And after the Mar-a-Lago Raid, America will never be the same. They do it through blackmail, whispered suggestions, bribery, and attacks on our liberty disguised as "woke" politics. The dark and demonic speech and setting by Brandon in Philadelphia was a stark statement of the battle lines in America. Fret not though - we are the majority.

Donors and lobbyists grant financial control over the party politics of our great nation's democratic structures, as is evidently clear to see in the impact of the eco-warriors on our politics.

Since the horrors of 9/11, it is clear to see that the corruption within our government extends far beyond policy formation. As I have highlighted, the relationship between law enforcement and intelligence has become an acutely intimate one—an intertwining that is so deep and entangled that they have become indistinguishable and are actively being used to control and repress society.

This relationship has not only a profound societal impact but an immense impact on the decisions our leaders make, even those who have been poisoned or corrupted. The decisions they make are done so based on the information that they have received. If this information is corrupted, or carefully selected at the source from institutions that are inherently trusted, then they are susceptible to poor decision-making through no fault of their own.

To add to the inescapable weight of influence is the role the Deep State plays in the military-industrial complex that makes ours the most powerful military in the world. Do I believe the US military is a willing servant to the Deep State? No. I truly believe, from firsthand experience, that our armed forces act with the interest of US citizens at heart. But do I believe that those who control the deployment of our armed forces are willing servants?

Yes. I absolutely do.

As such, the Forever War that our military is embroiled in does not benefit the United States but instead the pockets of those who sell the weapons and services. Those plutocrats who own our weapons manufacturers—and I am not just talking small or conventional arms—stand to gain immense sums of wealth and domination through the profligate of wars that never end.

Once again, from my own experience, the agents of the Deep State seep into the fabric of the Pentagon, spreading lies, poisoning minds, and bypassing tried and trusted security protocols to force through memorandums, policies, and actions that serve nobody but those looking to undermine our sovereignty from within.

On the surface, this may appear to be an unwinnable conundrum. Our enemies exert supreme influence on the foundations of our democracy at every level. Even the local level. But it is at this level that they can be beaten. At this level, the will of the people holds more sway and is more important than at every other level and arena of government. At the local level, we hold a microscope to the petri dish that is our local democracy. We know our communities, and we know when things are simply not right and do not add up.

We can see the corruption, we can feel it, and it is in this arena that we have the ability to gather support and challenge the enemy directly. Here, we can fight back against the Deep State, giving us the popular support and momentum to strike back in those upper echelons that feel so out of reach.

Big Academia

The next Corner of Deceit lies within the structures that inform and grow the next generation and alter the paradigms and perspectives of our direction of travel. Here, I am referring to Big Academia.

Through the influence of our educational apparatus, and the curricula that our children and our future leaders, thinkers, and innovators are subjected to, they cherry-pick and select the avenues of research that we as a society choose to embark upon, as well as the means upon which they are communicated.

As such, they are able to spread their lies and dogma as fact, guaranteeing willing compliance and subservience of the masses as they flock to these manufactured versions of the truth.

Those who present alternative conclusions are shunned, ostracized, and lambasted, and attacked both personally and professionally. Scientific rationalism is thrown away, under the guise of exactly that—scientific rationalism. Information is closely controlled, meaning that hypotheses are drawn and published from incomplete data sets presented as complete ones, whereas those who present conclusions from the complete sets of data are quickly overruled by the sheer weight of academics who are operating under the sway of the Deep State.

Once again, many of our educators do not even know that they are under the control of the elite, but their funding comes from somewhere, right?

That "somewhere" is the pockets of wealthy benefactors that keep the universities afloat and direct the course of study through the funding of very specific programs. And in our elite universities—the Ivy League—the children of the powerful elite flock to form the relationships that will form the cement that binds together the next generation of the Deep State.

And I hate to break it to you, but the everyday influence on our children that the Deep States craves already exists; it has wormed its way into schools at every level.

As corruption grows and manifests itself throughout government, it of course finds its way into the Department of Education. This department is the smallest of the Cabinet agencies. Shocking really, given how vital it is that we educate our children in the right way. Keeping the Department of Education small undoubtedly has its benefits. It is overworked, understaffed, and so the necessary due diligence on what should make it into the curriculum simply does not happen. This is how we end up teaching our kids about Critical Race Theory instead of proper Bible study.

The Department of Education also has a long list of secretaries and senior leadership figures who, prior to their appointment, had absolutely nothing to do with education. Many of these figures have been placed into these roles for explicitly political reasons, to push agendas and protect policies that otherwise would never see the light of day.

The result is a system of education that falls behind the educational institutions of many Western and Asian countries, where teachers are overworked, underpaid, and teaching a curriculum that holds society back instead of pushing it forward. And to be clear, America spends more on education per student than any country in the world. Where does this funding go? That's a great question. This is why there is a remarkable growth in homeschooling.

Once again, the amazing mothers of this nation know what is right for their kids, and they know that this failing educational system is not it.

Big Tech

Technology is taking over our lives. Look around you. How many devices do you have in your home? How many smart devices do you have? How many social media sites are you signed up to, and how many "free" games do you play on your phone?

I am going to begin this by saying that I do not for one second believe that technological advancement and adaptation is a bad thing. Because it simply is not. The power that our rapid growth in technology has to advance our species and master our surroundings cannot be understated. It is this growth that has led to amazing advances in healthcare, personal security, and allows us to communicate and seek the truth behind the lies.

The issue with this tech is the way that we, as people, have been commodified and turned into a product. You, your habits, and your data have been turned into data points that are sold to the highest bidder, which in turn is used to sell things to you and, more crucially, to control you.

It is no wonder that during the Arab Spring of 2011, the first thing those ailing governments did was switch off the internet. In Egypt, protesters communicated primarily through Twitter, communicating and coordinating their movements through Facebook events and tweets. When the government switched off the internet, they simply routed dial-up connections through Israel and continued to coordinate their movements. The internet is an extremely powerful tool for social mobility, and the Deep State knows this.

As a result, they use it to their own end. They harvest our data, carefully control the information that is disseminated through the mainstream platforms, and cram our feeds with junk content, all with the ultimate goal of limiting the true information that contradicts their agenda. To find this information, we have to actively go looking for it.

They use technology to sway public opinion and movement, rewriting societal norms and agendas to fit their desired narratives and sow discord and division throughout large swathes of society. And it is so easy for them because they put the devices in our homes and in our hands, putting the information they want us to see right at our fingertips.

If you disagree with the narratives they are looking to push, they own the platforms, so they simply remove you from them, banning your content in the process. Look at what happened with President Trump, and what has been happening with political commentators over the last five years as social media companies continually rewrite their algorithms to negatively impact those who are telling the truth!

This tech is also used to subvert our democracy. Look at the thousands of bot accounts that came out of Russia during the 2016 election, both in support of and in opposition to Trump. All these accounts sought to do was spread lies and confuse voters, rendering them inactive and uncertain of which way to vote.

The worst part of all of this is that we, as a society, have become dependent upon this tech. Sure, many of us actively use it against them, particularly on platforms like YouTube, but the point remains that we are still using the tech, and ultimately, they hold the power to pull the plug.

They hold the keys to medical advancements, they build the weapons and the countermeasures, and they fill our homes with devices that listen to us but that we are ultimately dependent upon.

It is a dangerous cocktail that, if we do not recognize its influence, has the potential to blind us and pull us gently into submission. However, if we recognize that those tools also have the power and the potential to uplift us and empower us, then we retain the ability to use them against them, using them as the tools of social mobilization that they were intended to be, but for our benefit.

Big Finance

The final Corner of Deceit is one that I know we are all aware of. It has been spoken of many, many times, and characterized by extreme wealth and the polarity of control when it comes to our financial institutions and those that operate globally.

The vast amount of global wealth is controlled by a tiny proportion of the global population, and these plutocrats hold all the keys. They control the flow of capital, lending and borrowing, and the selective dissemination of wealth throughout society.

The immense financial institutions that possess greater wealth than many small countries are all geared toward a stance that promotes globalization. For them, globalization is a good thing in that it removes many of the barriers that allow capital to flow freely throughout the world and, ultimately, back to them.

This serves a purpose that is greater than simple greed, holding such immense wealth guarantees immense power and influence. Just look at the role the World Economic Forum and the World Trade Organization play. When the euro almost collapsed in 2009–2010, the WTO seized the initiative and made it impossible for countries like Greece, Portugal, and Ireland to secure financial aid without integrating infrastructural change according to the designs of the WTO.

This led to the rise of technocratic regimes throughout Europe, where elected policymakers were overruled by technical "experts," each with their pockets loaded by WTO and WEF bureaucrats who aim to remove the barriers between nations.

Their view, in conjunction with the other Four Corners, is that they "know what is better" for society than sovereign, functional governments that put their own countries first. This was the essence of the Donald J. Trump thesis.

A "nation first" ethos is what every country should believe in: America First; Mexico First; Russia First; China First... Every nation should adopt a stance where the interest of their own citizens and sovereign territory is priority one. A sovereign national government is the best method of human governance. After all, we are tribal creatures, you need only look at the way we latch on to sports teams!

The worldwide governance that the WEF, the UN, and the EU are pursuing is not a means of governing that has our best interests at heart. The only people whose interests it serves are those who sit at the head of these worldwide governance structures, those who control all of the money.

We should reject a worldwide governance system where there is only one form of global governance. It is a slippery slope to global authoritarianism.

We should seek strength in functional governments that can provide for their countries and their people. There is nothing wrong with that. It is a good thing. What reminds me of that is how the elites hate the idea. They hate it because they want to rule on scale. It is easier to force us all to inject a vaccine that causes more harm than good when we have one form of government. It is easier to force us to reject our principles when there is only one form of government. This is why federalism works for us here in the United States.

What does a Portuguese career politician sitting in a UN office know about me? Nothing. Let the Portuguese take care of the Portuguese and let me take care of me.

This leads me to the UN—not so much a Corner of Deceit as it is a PR machine and the political arm of the global Deep State.

All of Which Leads to Globalism

Perhaps the most troubling thing about the Deep State is that it is not a uniquely American phenomenon. I have already allayed to you how it has long been an active feature of Turkish and Egyptian politics, and how globalists have engaged in a campaign of spreading its influence by eroding borders and attempting to transcend conventional geopolitics.

The best example of this is the United Nations. Spearheaded by President Woodrow Wilson as the League of Nations in 1918. The aim of this new multinational conglomeration of states was a security pact aimed at preventing the events of the Great War from happening again. It came from a set of noble ideals, but as it evolved into the UN, it has grown to become an obscene freak show of dysfunction.

Through this freak show, I have watched the shameful actions of retired military officers from other countries as they receive nice stipends from their governments while pocketing opulent salaries and compensations for working at the UN, spouting ludicrous insanity and utter nonsense. The UN has made a healthy income from lecturing people and has generously lined the pockets of those willing to sell their souls to join the circus.

The UN looks to reject and overrule constitutional governments because they believe that people are *too stupid to know what is good for them*. They sit on an ivory throne of perceived superiority and lecture us all on how borders are a bad thing, except for when it benefits them—Ukraine anyone!?

The UN is preposterous. They hold forums on women's rights and invite Syria and Iran—you know, those well-known advocates for the rights of women—and we are going to have a conference about counterterrorism that will be led by Libya and Syria? I mean, really? One of these nations has a long history of sponsoring global terrorism through its now dead, maniacal Islamic colonel and the other has been dropping gas on its own people for the last decade as it oppresses any notion of democracy. It is madness!

And it is no wonder that people are adding their weight to this madness. We need a forensic analysis of what and how these people are paid. It is no wonder that someone from Ghana or Burkina Faso wants to work at the UN. They can earn a fortune pushing complete nonsense across the world!

Me? I do not want that filthy lucre, it is shameful.

Me? I am a contrarian to all this silliness. I have both the right and the knowledge to question how we have evolved and promulgated theses on what we do about it. This is NOT what the Founding Fathers intended!

If people saw what truly goes on in these departments and agencies, they would see it for what it is: a racket disguised by tailored suits, photographed smiles, and handshakes.

It is called Critical Race Theory now, but in the '90s it was called "Sensitivity Training." At one such "Training Session" held in the late '90s when I worked in a federal agency, we were being lectured by a suit in a large conference room. Discontent and murmuring grew throughout the lecture as we were patronized and told to ignore common sense and rewire our thinking.

The murmuring and mumbling appeared to be coming from the far corner of the room, and as I turned in my seat to see where it was coming from, a group of Black Evangelicals arose from their seats as one, with one man shouting, "We're not going to be a part of this!" They ushered themselves from the room, taking dozens of people with them, and shut the session down.

They saw this progenitor to CRT for what it was, and what it still is. It is not about facts, it is about ideology, about swaying the masses into a collective way of thinking that shepherds the entire flock. These people know how to make a utopia. They know that collective messaging and false unity pave the way. Very bad things happen when you get people of wealth, status, and power attempting to establish utopia.

Do what those Evangelical men and women did, throw it out. This way of thinking is all part of the Deep State mindset. *If we had a little more power… a little more funding… we can make utopia work this time…* That is the logic of the Four Corners of Deceit.

These Four Corners of Deceit are the foundation of the Deep State. They are the solid basis from which they look to promote the control that they have over every aspect of our lives. The good news is that each of these Corners can also be used against them. We can take back control by starting at the local level, using it to undermine the global control that they seek.

We cannot compete with them at the global level, they are simply too powerful, but if we can seize local control, we can use this to mobilize millions of people and take back control as a single polity, operating under a constitutional government and not a global institution that hands true power to the few.

Chapter Nine
How Societies Collapse

"You don't understand the class structure of American society," said Smetana, "or you would not ask such a question. In the United States, the working class are Democrats. The middle class are Republicans. The upper class are Communists."

Whittaker Chambers

Boundaries are a good thing. Boundaries are what stop society from degenerating, and society is degenerating at a frightening rate. If you have no boundaries, you have no moral foundation.

The United States of America is a Judeo-Christian nation, and it is the Christian values enshrined in the Constitution that set the boundaries that have allowed our society to thrive and grow, becoming the most powerful and advanced nation on Earth in such a short time.

We now live in a time where people actively search for reasons to push the boundaries of society, all in the name of "societal progression." I believe that we should not seek progression for progression's sake. This is a dangerous tactic. Progression should always be aimed at advancing humanity, based upon a secure moral foundation: the one that exists in the Bible.

Progression for the sake of progression is a self-perpetuating cycle that has no end. A mission has arisen to challenge the boundaries that have allowed this nation to thrive, and in so doing, these "liberal philosophers" have made degeneration and debauchery perfectly acceptable. The boundaries that hold us together are fast eroding.

When there are no boundaries—when you *have* no boundaries—anything goes. And when anything goes, *anything goes.* Where does this end? Does it end when one recognizes sexual attraction toward children as a sexual orientation? If you think this is far-fetched, this rhetoric has already begun. Just look up pedophilia on Wikipedia and you will find the following quote:

"Pedophilia emerges before or during puberty, and is stable over time.[12] It is self-discovered, not chosen. For these reasons, pedophilia has been described as a disorder of sexual preference, phenomenologically similar to a heterosexual or homosexual orientation." [13]

Now, I know that Wikipedia is not the world's most reliable source, but it is one that millions of people turn to. It is the very definition of a mainstream knowledge base. This rhetoric is being spouted by academics and psychologists alike as they, in line with the Big Academia agenda, are incentivized to promote this degenerate behavior as genetic. You do not need to search very far to find this travesty being repeated.

This erosion of boundaries is why the leaders of globalism—crooks like Klaus Schwab, the leader and founder of the WEF—tell us to reject the notion that our children are our own and that they belong to society, that their purpose is to serve.

My advice in dealing with these crooks is not to engage. Do not rise to it. Do not try to dialogue with them. Do not even quibble with them. REJECT

---

12. https://en.wikipedia.org/wiki/Pedophilia
13. Cutler, Brian L., ed. (2008). "Pedophilia." Encyclopedia of Psychology and Law. Vol. 2. SAGE Publications, Inc. p. 549. ISBN 978-1-4129-5189-0.

IT. Reject it because what we know is that everything they believe in leads to the collapse of society.

"But how is that possible," you may ask, "when what they want to achieve is utopia?" Well, it is possible because the removal of boundaries and hyper-globalization leads to the demise of society, to the collapse of global order, and the moral/ethical desensitization of the human race.

When everything is on the table, nothing is off it.

Remember, we are dealing with those who have no moral foundation and hold an express desire to remove all rules and boundaries; they want to promulgate a utopia for us.

Professor Yuval Noah Harari, an Israeli historian and anthropologist, whose research centers on the progressive devolution of humanity based on technological and societal advancements, said in an article in the Guardian that "if governments and corporations succeed in hacking the human animal, the easiest people to manipulate will be those who believe in free will."[14] This is the man who is the chief advisor to Klaus Schwab!

We have to start the fight soon, for if we do not, the world will become brainwashed to the point that those who fight against the tide will be swept up by it, ostracized, and vilified into begrudging compliance. I do not know about you, but to me, this already hits dangerously close to home. To the elites, we are little more than servants, here to enact their will and redesign the world according to their image.

But what are the signs? How do we know that society is collapsing? What does history show us?

They Become Wealthy and Affluent

Straight off the bat, I want to start by telling you that I am a staunch capitalist. I do not believe that wealth and affluence are bad things. I believe that those

---

14.Harari, Yuval Noah (14 September 2018). "Yuval Noah Harari: the myth of freedom." The Guardian. The Guardian.

who work for what they have are entitled to it. It is in that type of society that we progress and that we progress based on societal and technological progression.

In a market economy, we are forced to continuously redesign, to innovate, and to create the next best thing. Just look at medicine or the home comforts that we surround ourselves with. Our televisions, our computers—our commodities. Look at those things that inherently change society, like the printing press or the internet.

What I *do* believe, though, is that wealth and affluence slow people down and is a highly effective tool of control and coercion. And once we have wealth, we will do anything we can to not lose it.

This is the story of colonialism. Those empires of immense wealth and power (Britain, Spain, France) developed empires that spanned the globe, and they did it to grow and preserve their wealth. They stole, enslaved, and murdered millions in the name of resource acquisition and competed in a global rat race that saw the birth of the largest empire the world has ever seen.

Indigenous people fought their wars, sold their neighbors, and farmed the land to fill the coffers of those who brought war to their shores—all because of the allure of wealth and fear-based oppression.

So many of these nations have failed to recover. Africa, Asia, and South America are littered with the remnants of colonialism, devastated by the legacy of imperial oppression.

And what happened to those empires? They all disappeared. Sure, the original countries remain, but they are not the global powers that they once were. They too have struggled to adapt since the fall of imperialism.

The influence of wealth and affluence and the degradation of society has two faces. The first of these is the ability to normalize and casualize human rights offenses. We can see this playing out in the Middle East and South America.

Countries in these parts of the world have hit the proverbial jackpot, sitting on immense deposits of oil and gas. These deposits have made the elite who own those deposits—the Al Saud family, for example—immensely wealthy and powerful, living with a freedom and a license to do whatever they please to whomever they please. They prop up those around them, making them wealthy, but this wealth depends wholly on protecting the wealth of their benefactors.

This creates an environment where the nation is ruled by a tiny yet immensely powerful elite but where the citizenry is abused, their human rights curtailed, with nobody willing or able to protect them.

It will be interesting to see what happens now to Chile. Chile is a country with an already tumultuous history of autocracy, recovering from a legacy that saw Augusto Pinochet habitually throw dissidents out of helicopters.

The government of Chile has recovered well and now sits on vast deposits of the biggest geological commodities since oil: copper and lithium. These two minerals are essential in the production of electrical components, and as the world moves away from fossil fuels, these minerals are rapidly growing in importance and value.

It will be interesting to see then, as a developing country, which way Chile will fall. Will it maintain its national identity and internal strength, or will it turn toward hubris and abuse? Worse yet, will the people of Chile lose the foundation upon which they currently sit?

They Lose Their Foundation

The second face of wealth-based societal collapse is far more insidious in nature. It is much less visible. In this face, that fabric that makes up the nation is subtly and gently ripped apart. This is the face that we see in the Western World.

In societies where there is plenty of wealth to go around, there is an immense risk of complacency and docile laziness. People become comfortable; life becomes effortless. When life becomes effortless, it is easy to settle for that to be happy with it. People express gratitude toward those who make life easy and effortless, and those people are those who hold the keys: the plutocrats, Silicon Valley, socialists…

These institutions create cults and monopolize innovation, using it as a means to control the flow of progress. They control the narratives that pervade society, that attack boundaries and ethics, and while the flag and the banner remain, the identity of the nation for which it stands disappears, replaced by something new and unidentifiable.

With its identity and its virtues lost, the society becomes a veritable hive of bedlam and debauchery, where common decency is replaced by "liberalism" and "wokeness." The Bible is thrown aside as society pulls away from God. Boundaries disappear, and supranational entities form, whose power supersedes that of the sovereign state. As more and more societies crumble, these entities take the reins, and society is softly and slowly lulled into subtle slavery.

This is the ultimate goal of the UN, of the WEF, and of the European Union, among the multitude of other pan-national agencies that have sprung up in every continent on the globe, from the World Health Organization to the World Trade Organization: a slow, peaceful descent into subservience.

And they have the patience to get it done. They have been at this for decades, centuries even. The problem is, we are now dangerously close to the tipping point. Society is falling at an ever-increasing rate. The authority of the national institutions that have protected us up to now is beginning to evaporate as more and more crucial decisions are taken away from us.

The Brits saw this and woke up to it. Brexit was a movement that allowed the people of the United Kingdom to take control back from an organization that exacted a heavy financial toll and in return took away their ability to make crucial sovereign decisions and exercise control over their domestic and foreign policies.

They are not the only ones to have begun to awaken to the gradual disappearance of national sovereignty under the European Union. Euroskepticism is growing throughout Europe, with movements arising most prominently in the Netherlands, France, and Eastern and Southern Europe.

What they lack, though, is momentum. As the narrative continues to be determined by those who hold the power, populism and common sense are washed away by the wave of fake news and overbearing defamation in the media.

These political movements speak to the national values and foundations that made their nations great, and these narratives are drowned out by "progressives" who seek global governance. It is our responsibility to help give them a voice and to fight nonsense with common sense.

This fight, though, is exhausting.

They Lose Their Drive

Ask yourself: What are you passionate about? What one thing will you sacrifice anything for? Why is it that you are willing to sacrifice everything for this one thing?

Often, the answer to this is children, family, loved ones. It is very rare that these things are material. They, far more often than not, relate to people. They relate to people because the people we love are what we cannot imagine living without.

For many, the answer to the question *what would you die for?* is their country. This answer happens when the country relates to something far more than soil, land, or territory. It happens when, to us, our country is home; it is what keeps our families safe and secure, and it represents something that we intrinsically believe in.

I know this because my country is something I would gladly die for, as it is for anybody who has served. This is because I truly love my country. I love what it stands for, what it represents, and what it protects. This is why I have devoted my life to service to my country.

I have also devoted my life to God. God is my light and my beacon, and it is in service to Him that I have dedicated my life to protecting freedom and liberty throughout the world.

Religion and belief, as we know, are highly motivating factors. In answer to that question, many would say that they would die for their faith. Where faith is the cornerstone of the nation, it enhances the sense of national self-identity. We see this all over the world, especially in the Middle East.

The United States of America is a Christian nation. It is this faith that has granted our nation God's favor and that has guided us through the rapid growth that has seen our country grow to be the greatest in the world.

The problem is that faith is in decline. As the Deep State strengthens its grip, more and more people are turning away from faith as the boundaries that once kept us secure are being broken down and torn apart.

As this happens, the foundations that construct the very fabric of society are reduced to rubble, and the values that make us inherently American no longer matter. The family unit is more divided and at risk than ever before, and Christian values mean less to society than they ever have.

This makes two things happen. Firstly, the general will and momentum to fight back disintegrates or is replaced by a sedate "happiness" that leads to a false sense of security. This happens when comfort is achieved. Often, people turn to God when things are difficult or challenging. They take comfort for granted, forgetting to be thankful for their comfort, and instead conveniently exercise their belief in God only when they need someone to blame or to help.

And the same is true of the nation. As so many Americans—and citizens from other nations in the developed world—live lives of increased comfort and ease, they forget to engage with society and only become politically active when that comfort is at risk or pulled away.

The second thing that happens is conflict. This conflict occurs between those who reject the life that the Deep State has crafted for us—refusing to bow to their will or demands and devote their lives to God and their nation—and those who have submitted, caught up in the current of the crumbling society that the Deep State has created.

These brave patriots will fight tooth and nail to preserve the way of life that sets healthy boundaries and provides the security that guarantees them and, most importantly, their children safety, security, and opportunity.

This is what we are now seeing here in the United States. It is the reason this book, and so many others like it, have been written.

This fight, though, is exhausting. It is like swimming upstream through rapids, getting buffeted and battered by the water and the rocks that is the devolved "society" and their mockery and insults.

Here, it is only too easy to give up, to surrender the fight, and join the crowd. The true heroes, those who are still fighting, know that God, the nation, and the rescued society will thank them for their efforts in the long-term, and they will be rewarded by the resurgence and the rebirth of the nation.

When they can see the shift in momentum, and their eyes are opened, the comfort blanket that has blinded them will be whipped away, and they will realize that their freedom has been stolen slowly, gradually, but undeniably.

Once this happens, they will join the fight. And it all starts at the local level.

Chapter Ten

A Return to Election Integrity

"The secret of freedom lies in educating people, whereas the secret of tyranny is in keeping them ignorant."

Maximilien Robespierre

At the beginning of this book, I promised you an action briefing. I promised, using my experience, knowledge, and credentials, to lay out the framework for how we take back control, starting at the local level. I purposed myself after the disastrous 2019 Virginia elections to teach myself about the election process in America. I realized that many politicians and self-declared experts do not understand the process of elections in their counties and states—shocking but true. The reality is that many are far more concerned with fundraising than winning. Fundraising is better when you lose, and the Republican side of the Uni-Party often likes to occupy this revenue opportunity.

The reason I placed a microscope on Loudoun County is that Loudoun County is a place that sits close to my heart. I live very close by in Prince William County, but Loudoun is ground zero of the (peaceful) Citizen

Uprising in America. Sure, there are other counties across the country that have acted in a similar manner, that have taken a stand. But the citizens of Loudoun County, normally the example of a peaceful American society, have been in an absolute uproar.

They are in an uproar because they typify the American values that we hold so close to our hearts, and their social sensibilities and typically reserved nature has given way to outrage and action.

I have sat close to this action, provided briefings, and helped lay the foundations of a movement that challenges election integrity and seeks to preserve it.

For decades, Americans assumed that "someone else" was taking care of elections, trusting that our votes would be put to use in the right way and serve as our voice in the formation of our governments.

In 2020, we learned, undeniably, that someone else really was taking care of elections, and it was not someone to be trusted. Loudoun County, and so many others, watched as traditional voting gave way to travesty, as though their political affiliations suddenly performed an about-face.

And in many counties, just like Loudoun, this change happened over the course of several years, several election cycles. Demographics did not change, opinions remained the same, and even gubernatorial elections demonstrated the traditional political affiliations, but somehow, federal elections all seem to have moved in one direction.

This is how, despite the fact that Biden won in the presidential election in Loudoun, Republican Glen Youngkin was elected Governor of Virginia—the first Republican governor in the state since 2009—where Loudoun represented one of the driving factors in this victory and, once again, voted Republican despite apparently voting for "no inflation in July" Joe. Moms, parents, and pastors led the massive turnout in Virginia. Terry McAuliffe, Youngkin's opponent, still won Loudoun, Arlington, Prince William, and the all-important Fairfax County (the Fulton County of Virginia) but energized turnout in these counties aided the outlying counties in outvoting these suspect counties.

It took Communist Steve McClure eleven years (2008–2019) to flip Virginia from Red to Blue. It will take time for citizens to reassert control of their counties and states. If we fail to address this imbalance, then the direction that this will take us in is one that takes us away from our traditional values, from sense and sensibility, and toward societal decay and global governance. If it carries on, then eventually the question *what does it mean to be American?* will have no valid answer.

Give Me the Mic!

To seize control, we have to shape both the conversation and the outcome. To do this, we have to be heard; we have to grasp the opportunity to speak whenever we are given the opportunity. We have to spread our message, unflinchingly, forsaking gentle civility and rocking the apple cart.

We have to take to county councils, school board meetings, town halls, anything that has an audience where we cannot be stifled by the bureaucrats who have been elected to these positions. Every time there is an "Open Mic" session where citizens are allowed to share public comments, YOU MUST BE THERE!

Even in a peaceful democracy, governance is a contact sport. If you say you are a Constitutional Conservative and are not happy with the direction of the country, you must make time to appear at these sessions. Grab the mic (having already done some basic research so you can speak with authority) and let it rip!

I have, as a result, found myself taking to all kinds of forums and stages to rip into the machine that threatens to corrupt the inner and outer workings of our democratic processes. Recently, I gave sworn testimony in a federal hearing, and when asked about the 2020 election, I gave the following response: "We have a sworn president. His name is Joe Biden, and the process has run its course. I do think we have questions with our election process, and I believe it's reasonable to look into them."

This response appeared to unsettle the cross-examining attorney. I used a mic opportunity to say that these matters are not mutually exclusive. You can have both situations at the same time, and it is likely the first time he had ever heard this line of reasoning.

Seize Your Mic Opportunity

On another occasion, I remember sitting in my office when my phone started ringing. The number was a familiar one, an old friend, now a mayor in New Jersey who has broken a forty-two-year stranglehold by a corrupt Blue machine. A powerful, Wall Street lawyer who has been blessed while unequivocally advocating the conservative cause. On this occasion, he was fighting the politicization of prejudice.

"John, would you be able to attend my next city council meeting?" he asked me. To me, this was another opportunity to grab the mic.

"Absolutely, how can I help?" I asked, curious to see what he had planned.

"I'm holding a city council meeting next week, and I was hoping you would come to the virtual meeting. Can you do that?"

This is just the opportunity I needed, another platform on which to make some noise and highlight the ways in which positive messages are politicized and used to divide and polarize rather than unite and enact positive change.

So I attended, and the virtual meeting was a full house. The mayor recognized me, and I opened the floodgates for thirty minutes, lifting the lid on Critical Race Theory, Black Lives Matter, and the way the fight for equality has been hijacked and commandeered by those looking to cause division. This is something that Ann Vandersteel, who I will tell you all about later, has reinforced in her many podcasts and speaking engagements; BLM and ANTIFA have been weaponized to halt the court of public opinion.

"It is shameful," I told them, "that we have a system and a model that teaches kids to hate their brethren and their country! It is disgraceful that we allow this to continue, that we pretend that we are doing it for the sake of 'decency,' when instead all we are doing is allowing those with no vested interest in the agenda to sabotage it to their own end, weaponizing it to undermine the freedom and liberty that this nation was established to defend!"

The room was, as was expected and desired, torn between a state of shock and disbelief. For many, I had said what they were thinking but did not have the courage to say. For others, I was saying something that verged on political blasphemy, that confronted their prejudices and laid them bare for all to see. No one had dared challenge these high priests of social purity before.

For those, it was too much to bear, and many of them left the meeting. Some of them never came back, which helped to remove a degree of the opposition that was making it difficult for him to serve his city.

His key battle mirrors that of many other cities and counties in twenty-first century America: the collusion of county and city councils to allow big hedge funds like Black Rock to essentially, through a veil of smoke and mirrors, fund the purchase on scale of property for development purposes. By development, I mean the construction of gigantic apartment blocks and condos to force people to live in cramped living spaces en masse.

Why is this an important battle? Because people, when crammed and stuffed together into communal living spaces, act differently. Community spirit disappears as people become territorial over their space.

Such conditions grant those in power societal control and limit the mobility and diaspora of populations, herding the people into easy-to-control bubbles. It is also lucrative. Building upward limits the amount of space needed, and "affordable housing," with people piled on top of each other, means that developers can maximize the revenue generated per square foot. And all of this money goes straight into the pockets of the elites in the perfect racket: control and wealth.

This is part of the Swamp everybody has to deal with on a daily basis across the country. While I am dealing with the Deep State in DC, everybody else has to deal with the Deep State where they live (and I do eat my own dog food and spend time pressuring my own county apparatus). This is the tangible Deep State people feel on their doorstep, intruding upon every part of our lives.

Local Civilian/Citizen/Patriot POWER: The Loudoun County Effect

The county is the foundation of our Republic. I have said it many times over, and I will say it many times more. We cannot hope to take back control if we focus our efforts on DC; the corruption is too deep and the corruption begins and is based upon loss of control of our counties, towns, and cities.

Loudoun County, though, is closer to DC than the enemy would like. Despite their attempts to soften Loudoun, to change the fundamental demographics that make up the county, it is still fighting back, and the message is seeping through into neighboring counties.

This is because nothing can repress the Patriot Power that exists within the DNA of Loudoun County, and that is embedded within every county, albeit deeper in some than others.

I have spent many hours, days, weeks, and months since the events of 2020 supporting the people of Loudoun, offering my voice and my expertise, providing strategic insight in dismantling the machine based on my almost forty years of experience.

What I have learned, and what I have taught, is there are four things that make up the foundation of our country at the local level, and it is in challenging these four things that will provide a direct challenge to the authority of the Deep State.

In Virginia and all states and territories (there are roughly 3,300 or so counties or county equivalents), these same, common four cornerstones are:

- The County Council
- The Election Board
- The Registrar
- The School Board

These four elements control local policy, election integrity and efficacy, and the education that we provide to our children. The four cornerstones are not enough alone, though, for the Deep State to hold control and for us to take it back. They need grounding and support. This comes from:

- The Sheriff
- District Judges/Clerk of the Court
- State Attorney (in Virginia called the Commonwealth Attorney)

These three additional pillars provide the legal backing and "legitimacy" that the Deep State uses as a sword to legitimize the crimes it perpetuates every day. I call these seven common groups the Seven Centers of Gravity. These are the foundation of governance in our Constitutional Republic. By taking back control of the Centers of Gravity at the local level, we are able to directly challenge the Deep State at the national level by whipping away their support from right under their feet and deploying it for ourselves against them.

The titles, roles, and missions of these Centers of Gravity may vary from state to state, but the responsibilities will look largely the same, so identifying who holds similar responsibilities is crucial.

But what does that fight look like? What are the logistics? What actions can you take?

The first task is to know the numbers. Know your numbers and know your citations. This is vital because you maintain integrity. You have to know what integrity looks like and, most importantly, what it does not.

The numbers you need to know are:

1. Election Numbers: What were the vote counts for Candidates A, B, and so on? What were the early vote numbers and percentages? What about the "drop off" numbers and percentages?
2. The total numbers for A+B? The early voting numbers for A+B?
3. Early voting categories in the state?
4. Early voting period in the state?
5. Precincts in the county?
6. Early voting numbers in the county in 2020, 2021, and so on?
7. What trend lines exist?
8. The state election code?

By forensically analyzing these numbers and committing them to memory, you have all you need to identify any disturbing trends and numbers that seem out of place or downright suspicious. For example, in Prince William County, the 2021 election winner saw an early voting percentage of 45 percent of their total vote, with the losing candidate only receiving 34 percent of their votes as early votes.

To speak with authority on the situation in your county or county equivalent, you must know these basics. I have had many well-meaning patriots who are very upset with issues in the 2020 election (as am I) yet know nothing about their own county in regard to the 2020 numbers (when asked if Trump won or lost their county in 2020, almost everyone has said they do not know—step 1 before a jot or tittle of anger or emotion—know your numbers).

There Is No One Else, There Is Only Us

Next, let's discuss the *in front of the counter* and the *behind the counter* actors when it comes to the election process. Think of this as a store. In front of the counter, you have customers, product/service users, and you have authorities that are designed to keep the shop compliant, like mystery shoppers and inspectors.

In this scenario, the customers are us, the voters. We use the service, we cast our ballots, and we expect a level of integrity and effectiveness in return, *behind the counter.* We expect that our votes count as we intended them to and that the ultimate outcome is the one that is fair and accurate according to the vote.

You also have poll watchers. These are volunteers who monitor the polls and the election facilities. Often, these are there at the behest of the parties, and they have the job of reporting or lifting the lid on disparities and suspicious practices.

Behind the counter, we have the store clerks, the folks who stack the shelves, count the money, and ensure that the store runs effectively. In the case of elections, these are the sworn election officers, whose role, mandated by oath, is to run the elections. Most of them are temporary—they are essentially deputized citizens, sworn in to run the elections. What this means is that anyone can perform this role. They are in charge of voter registration, foreseeing potential issues regarding the fairness and integrity of the election, and protecting the democratic rights of voters. They are also responsible for the information campaigns prior to the election, and they have the ability to determine how many people vote and in what manner according to whatever agenda they push prior to the election.

Who do you think has more influence on the outcome of the election?

That's right! It is those folks who sit behind the counter, and there is growing evidence that this group of people is increasingly influenced by political agendas and donations, many of which come from leftist groups with "progressive" agendas.

In addition, there is rarely a party equivalence among the number of volunteers; it is almost always skewed quite dramatically in one direction. You would think there would be some form of vetting process to ensure the parity of volunteer political allegiances, whose vested interest is to prevent the other side, through a process of collaboration, from impacting the election. At least in Virginia, this is not Democrats acting mischievously, this is largely Republicans failing to volunteer and get engaged behind the counter. In the November 2021 Virginia election, there was much greater involvement by Republicans but still many reports of Republicans not providing constant coverage or being present during the voting process. In other states, there is mischievous behavior, and Republicans are usually the ones caving and folding.

I want to tell you the story of Clerk Tina Peters.

Tina hails from Mesa County, Colorado. She is courageous, brave, and is the prime example of a woman who is leading the fight for the control of her county. Tina possesses a determination to guarantee fair and free elections and has committed her life to the cause, to the extent that she signed up to be an election officer and is now running on the ballot for secretary of state in Colorado.

Service to the nation runs in the DNA of her family. You see, Tina is a Gold Star Mom, meaning that she understands better than anyone the pain of loss through sacrifice in service to the country. I admire and respect her for that.

But her troubles did not end there. In her duty as an election officer, Tina regularly reported inconsistencies and suspicious behavior, from people engaging in suspicious behavior to software updates that wiped election data. She appealed to local members of the GOP, whereupon she was immediately rejected and cast aside. This has led to her conviction that Deep State infiltration is not a strictly Democratic Party issue but that the GOP has been infiltrated too.

And there is certainly evidence to back this up! Her county is a very Red county, so for her to be lambasted and attacked in the way that she was flies in the face of logic. This attack grew so serious that she was arrested and charged with fraud, even spending time in jail with a half-a-million-dollar bail, which is unheard of in such a case. Even murderers do not get that.

The charges related to what was alleged incorrect practice regarding the use of monitoring and recording equipment, from which she was later cleared. That sham represented an ill-gotten attempt at removing her from her position as election officer. It was an attempt to prevent her influence from spreading to other election officers, which would ultimately lead to even greater election scrutiny.

The campaign against her did not end there. While she was being held, a coordinated attack against her way of life was orchestrated. Her father tragically passed away, and she was unable to go to her family in their, and her, time of need. In a further cruel twist, her house was raided by the FBI, who tore through her personal effects, including the effects of her late son.

Finally, her husband, suffering from dementia and Parkinson's, was convinced to sign a divorce decree from his bed in a nursing home, ending her marriage. Her action, and her advocacy, led to a wholesale attack against her. All she demanded was transparency, and all the Deep State proved was that it had something to hide.

Amazingly, none of this has dissuaded her. She is a hero, an inspiration, because she has not allowed this to defeat her. She has continued her campaign for secretary of state in Colorado. In the primary, an unknown, Deep State Republican funded by Mark Zuckerberg came out of nowhere to "beat" Tina.

But Tina is unstoppable—she has raised the funds for a recount[15] to look into this matter. All she needs now is the active support of like-minded citizens. Together, we are strong.

Together, we shield one another from the machinations of the Deep State.

15.https://www.thegatewaypundit.com/2022/07/will-bring-evil-empire-huge-update-candidate-tine-peters-raises-funds-recount-stolen-colorado-primary-race-incredible-achievement/

Chapter Eleven

Taking Back Control

"The most important office, and the one which all of us can and should fill, is that of private citizen."

Louise Brandeis

I am going to start this chapter with an uncomfortable truth; as the erosion of society has accelerated, so has the audacity of the Deep State. In my opinion, society has been primed and globalization has grown to the level that the United States is almost ripe for the taking, and it is my belief that we are dangerously close to witnessing the beginnings of the Deep State Takeover.

The Deep State has a hardcore view of how they want to control society. The thing is, they have had to be careful about how they have trodden until they feel that they have achieved a decisive level of control. They have had to be nuanced. This is where Critical Race Theory has come from.

We, the fighters, the warriors, are the reason that they have had to tread carefully. We have been lifting the lid on their activities with renewed gusto since 2016—since a US president actively joined the fight and promised to drain the Swamp.

If 2016 slowed them down, then 2020 sped them up.

The Beginnings of the Deep State Takeover

In 2020, the Deep State leveraged a virus for societal control en masse. Yes, the COVID-19 pandemic was a global pandemic, but have no doubt, COVID-19 was a broad strategic effort by China to replace the United States using all forms of warfare. We were, without doubt, the target. The rest was collateral.

2020 ushered in a new form of biological warfare. Biological warfare was often the topic of sci-fi, reserved for fiction. We never truly believed that it could be achieved. We feared smallpox and Ebola, but not a form of SARS. Coronavirus was the perfect weapon; not deadly enough to wipe out populations (making it easy to control and minimize the blowback) but sufficiently dangerous to vulnerable people so as to enforce protective measures and declare a global crisis.

The freakout over Wuhan was pure theater leveraged by the elites, the globalists, and World Economic Forum. Yes, Bill Gates was talking about a virus long before this, but that does not mean that Gates engineered the accidental release from Wuhan.

Matt Truong, a friend and former congressional candidate (who, by the way, was the walking example of "every vote counts" when he lost his nomination by five votes), talks about how the pandemic was used to remove the legislative and social impediments to the spread of Marxism and communism here in the United States.

He argues that the restrictions brought about by the pandemic accelerated and legitimized a decline in societal standards and legislative responsibility/ protection. Through forced vaccinations and restrictive policies, the power and the authority of the family unit are overruled, with the state replacing the parent as the supreme authority in our children's lives.

"These are the intermediate steps to Marxism, socialism, and, dare I say it, communism. There is no God, there is no higher being, there are no parents. All you have got is the Party. Here, parents will not have a say with their children, and the children will be segregated. COVID-19 allows the cabal to implement their socialism."

As Vietnamese Americans, Matt and his parents know better than most what this looks like. His community, and many Latin American and Chinese American communities, know very well what this looks like. And yet the power of the cabal is such that they are able to convince these families and these communities that this peaceful transition to Marxism is in their best interest. That it is desirable.

He reminds me and any who are active in the fight that we can turn the tide by better engaging these communities. For example, in his county of Fairfax, Virginia, and the wider Eleventh Congressional District, 19 percent of the population is Vietnamese American. This number, if effectively engaged and reminded of the horror of life under communist authoritarianism, can play an integral role in recognizing and combating the signs of rampant socialism.

What he tells me is that those people are starting to come around. They have been awakened by November 2020 and the events since, seeing the parallels between what they remember and what they are seeing now. These Vietnamese Americans, Chinese Americans, and Latino Americans are once again living what they escaped from. And so are their children.

Matt is another of the brave soldiers leading the fight against the Deep State. He has been active on social media, creating interest groups and creating communities from those who oppose the spread of cabalistic socialism.

He helped to begin the movement that found its way to Loudoun County from its roots in Fairfax. In Loudoun, the movement gained recognition, developed traction and volume, but its roots can be found in Fairfax. Matt is a member of the Coalition of Thomas Jefferson, a group of parents committed to rooting out improper practices in our schools at the school board level.

At one stage, this group was comprised of a membership of approximately 70 percent Asian Americans. Over time, wider membership has grown, with wider groups of society joining the group. Accordingly, the ratio of Asian American membership has dropped to 40 percent, such is the rate of increased social inclusion and growth. This group has successfully won several lawsuits against schools and the school board. Of course, the Left does not like this and has attempted to repress this information in an active attempt at trying to fight back, with no success.

In 2019, the Chinese laid out all their plans for warfare. The Chinese played the world lockdown extremely well. The world overreacted and freaked out, and we quickly learned who was a constitutionalist and who was a control freak. The Deep State was able to use legitimacy to override and strip away our liberty, confining us to our homes and forcing us to stick needles into our arms containing only God knows what. At least, those of us who have not resisted.

The virus allowed us to learn about the crazies in the public school system, those whose secret desire is for control, and those who want to use the government to oppress the population.

In 1999, the Chinese revealed their plan in a book called *Unrestricted Warfare*. In this book, two air force senior colonels in the People's Liberation Army highlighted the strategies through which they believed that China could destroy America, specifically under the pretext of globalization.

From this, it was clear that the Chinese read everything that we put out, they took note, and they knew precisely what to use against us and how to use it.

In my time in government, I have been witness to multiple Chinese hacks within our cyber infrastructure. The most notable was after the infamous Sony emails incident, where a large number of emails were leaked out of Sony in an aggravated response to the upcoming film *The Interview*, a parody about an assassination attempt on Kim Jong-un.

In these emails, Sony executives based out of Culver City, California, were caught red-handed talking racist trash about Obama. This led to complete chaos within the US government as we scrambled shortly later in our attempts to figure out what we were supposed to do when China struck with the largest cyber breach in history into the Office of Personnel Management.

Through this open act of warfare, they were able to access over 21 million files on anybody who had ever held a government security clearance or who had ever been a government employee.

Obama's people were furious but feckless. They were furious with China but were reticent to do anything about it. It was a response typified by inaction, oddly reminiscent of the 2022 crisis in Ukraine.

The easy, subtle response was to identify ways to inflict cost on China, just as we did with Russia through sanctions and trade embargos. Despite this, they demonstrated a sheer reluctance, too afraid of the political and economic repercussions. Sure, there were discussions. They asked me to produce a plan to inflict costs on China. I was thoroughly rejected. Every measure was deemed over-the-top, too provocative, and unacceptable. Yet somehow, a mass break-in data breach was perfectly fine! Not at all provocative!

So, instead of receiving the assurances that our government was willing to fight to defend our rights and liberties, people were instead lullabied into inaction by QAnon. QAnon, and other such people, aimed at making people active but instead rendered them inactive. They told scary bedtime stories and told the masses that the "plan" would take care of this, lulling those who oppose the Deep State into a false sense of security in the belief that everything was in hand.

I admire that these guys mean well, and they are on our side of the ledger, but Q turned people inactive not active.

I tell people over and over not to believe in a plan but to instead get involved in their county, to go to county board meetings, election board meetings, and school board meetings. You have to understand the topics, dominate them, and not let elites serve you their group psychosis.

Focus on *your* county. Yes, in DC, Pennsylvania, and in many other counties and areas within the country, they are stealing elections. We know, we get it, but you have to remember to ignore these and worry, for now at least, about YOUR COUNTY. Focus all your time and effort on your county. Control your county and the nation will follow.

Do not rely on the military to save you, the way that Q and the others tell you that they will. We have a major problem with senior uniformed leadership. The simple fact is that we cannot count on many of our senior officers anymore.

No, the way to break the bondage is to use the example given to us by the Loudoun County moms through their action, passion, and activism within the county.

Seize the microphone at every open mic session and let rip. Let them have it. Reveal the uncomfortable truths. Let them know we are onto them, inspire and drum up support from those who have been nullified into inaction.

Ann Vandersteel is one of the amazing women I have spoken of in this book. You may recall that I briefly mentioned her in relation to bringing to light the weaponization of positive intentions. She is an activist and a thought leader in her county and is an amazing example of someone who believes in taking back the country from what she calls the "dog-level of the Republic."

She identifies as an American State National, rejecting the Fourteenth Amendment that created the federal system that usurped our rights as mandated by God and created what she calls a corporate government. As she puts it, we have had our liberties revoked in exchange for privileges, and it is due to these privileges that we owe a debt to our government that steals our God-given liberty.

She rejects, overwhelmingly, the oppression of a political system that creates debt financially and socially, favoring instead the Founding Fathers' conception of a Union of States, not a centralized government.

It is a long-held belief of mine that many citizens, principally those who identify as liberal, do not realize that they have been weaponized, and it is now these folks who have blindly followed every governmental whim and are now dropping dead in airports because they blindly trusted a vaccine. This is view that Ann shares.

Most importantly, she posits, just like me, that the World Economic Forum and their allies are comfortable with the actions that they commit to and espouse because they do not believe in God. This lack of virtue and belief in eternal life drives them to actions that are immoral, and their fear of death, as a result, leads to them taking every action to strengthen themselves and their allies. So, we need to use God to fight them.

Christine Reagan from ACT for America also highlights the importance of using our faith in God as our weapon, saying that "God looks for people who are willing to finish the task before them." What she is referring to here is the need for us to see this out to the end, to fight against the adversity, and to use faith as the shield and the driving force that deflects distraction and inaction and drives us toward action and change. If we are relentless, God will reward us with blessings of opportunity to do more good.

She is more entitled than most to make this claim. As the National Director for ACT, she worked raising a young child and managing a household to create an organization that stands up relentlessly for the freedom of America. After 9/11, she recognized the weaponization of Islam and challenged the spread of Islamism on school campuses. And she has committed to a life of motivating action in as many people as she can in everything she does. "If we don't all step up and find that little corner where we can all step up… if we don't care, then we don't deserve a nation to begin with."

For her, the first radical thing that you can do is something you can actually do from the couch: pick up the phone and speak to the government.

Then, get involved in your house of worship. Put feet to your prayer. Work with your congregation on action in your community. Through a return to our Christian values (and fully realizing we are a diverse nation with multiple faiths), God will grant us the strength and unity to battle our enemies. We know this works. Remember, in the American Revolution, only 3 percent fought, and only 10 percent supported them, but of this 10 percent, a huge number were pastors, who rallied their congregations and created a surging wave of popular support and, most importantly, *action*.

The County Is the Center of Gravity

In the previous chapter, I spoke about the importance of knowing your numbers and understanding who and what to challenge. But it is not enough to just know, we have to follow up this knowledge with action.

So, Colonel Mills, what do I do now? What action do I take?

I promised you an action briefing. I promised to lay out the steps that you can take to guarantee fair elections in your county and to challenge unfairness.

The first step is a personal one. You need to be organized. You need to apportion time and purpose yourself. Check your diary, know your calendar, know what is happening and where. It is as imperative that you understand your goal. What is it that you want? If you are going to a board meeting, what are you looking for? What do you want to challenge? What do you want to change and challenge? What are your tactics?

There is no better place to spot election malpractice than as an election officer, so volunteer, nominate yourself, become a sworn election officer like Ann Vandersteel. From this platform, you are perfectly placed to spot things.

Once you are in place, it is time to engage the detective in you, to unleash your inner Sherlock Holmes and relentlessly challenge anything that is not right. The general rule of thumb is *if it does not feel right, it probably isn't*. So, challenge that which does not feel right, or okay, or legitimate. First, there are the obvious things, like thumb drives removed from polling machines, meaning that votes are not being recorded. Worse yet, who has that thumb drive? What are they doing with it?

Or if the poll books suddenly undergo a software update during polling times, which absolutely should not happen. The machines are formatted and prepared in advance, and there should be no last-minute changes on polling day that result in the need for an update. This is an indication that someone, or something, has accessed the machine remotely and should be investigated.

Double-check the signature requirements on mail-in/drop-off votes and ensure your colleagues know that the requirements are on these. Reject votes that do not have two signatures. These are invalid votes, and while some may be innocent mistakes, the sheer level of these that went under the radar in 2020 indicates an immense gap in the training or, in a more sinister twist, a combination of voter fraud and election officers turning the other cheek.

Keep an eye on the voter registrations too. Are they legal? Are they lawful citizens, are they of age, are they legally registered to vote? The last thing we want is the same faces turning up at multiple polling stations and casting multiple votes.

So, let us say you have spotted any of the above or you have seen things slipping through the net from other election officers. What do you do next?

This question has two answers. First, demand an on-the-spot vote and ensure that you trace it to the relevant election code. This is the quickest way to ensure fairness and stop fraud in its tracks.

You should only need to do this once. Once should be enough to scare them off and prevent anything nefarious from happening again. News will quickly spread to other polling stations, and if we have strength in numbers, and we are organized, then we can act as one to prevent the poison from spreading throughout the county.

The next thing is to have an affidavit prepared and to know where to take it in the event that you need to use it. Generally speaking, the sheriff or prosecutor should be the first port of call, and if we have managed our Centers of Gravity well, then they will be responsive to your admonitions. And take note, should you need to use your affidavit, make sure that you bring it to the sheriff within twenty-four hours so that it can be actioned on time before the damage is done.

For all of this to work, there is a level of preparation to do beforehand, so you need to ensure that you have your ducks in a row. I have also already alluded to the strength that we have in numbers, so seize the initiative and pull together a network of like-minded citizens, many of whom will be neighbors. Our army is the one that we send to the polling stations. Our uniform is the lanyard or the badge that declares our status as election officers. Train each other in what to look for and what actions to take so that our army acts as a well-oiled machine.

Most importantly, be brave. Be strong. Be ready and willing to fight.

Get Off the Couch and Get in the Game

If you follow these steps on election day, then your actions will go a long way toward ensuring a fair election. And if you spot and challenge attempted election fraud, malfeasance, or nonadherence to election law, that's a good thing. It means we have caught them red-handed, and we can make noise, shout, and scream, invigorating and energizing those who think like we do or have buried their heads in the sand. Bring them into the daylight. Allow them to see with the clarity that we do.

But this is just the beginning of the battle. What comes next is the strategizing, the grinding down, the daily fight that brings people to our cause while whittling away at the false legitimacy and veil that protects the Deep State.

You need to dominate the Centers of Gravity in your state, identifying who they are, their histories, and their political allegiances. Refuse to sit down and shut up. Be seen, be heard, attend the meetings, write often, challenge everything. Do what the amazing women of Loudoun County have been doing and speak up in council meetings, school board meetings, and be seen and filmed doing it!

Demand accountability for unlawful registrations. Challenge their origin and demand that authorities trace them back. And do not allow inaction to fester. Challenge that too. *Why has this not been followed up? Why aren't you doing your job?*

Demand clean voter rolls, and while you're at it, demand access to voter rolls. We deserve transparency! This is a democracy; what right have they got to keep secrets from us?

And whatever you do, *do not be afraid to name and shame.* Those who have deliberately tampered with our democratic processes are traitors, and they deserve to be treated as such. The public deserves to know who these traitors are. Your willingness to name and shame will ripple outward, and this ripple will grow into a wave that will scare away the traitors. Your action will drive them into inaction.

For our efforts to be successful, we need you, the citizen. The price of freedom is not only overseas with our military, it is at home with you—there is no one else to fight for your county but you.

There is no silver bullet.

There is no one else.

There is only you and your fellow citizens.

It is a long, grinding slog. It will take steel resolve to deliver election integrity.

Our political institutions were designed to oppose tyranny, to make radical change difficult to enact with thorough checks and balances or due diligence. This is why it has taken the Deep State so long to act as they have. It is also why we have to fight tooth and nail to overturn the damage already done and to prevent any further damage from occurring because our very system is designed to make it hard to reverse.

Welcome to our Constitutional Republic, the worst form of government in the world—except for every other form of governance. It was Winston Churchill who said, "Democracy is the worst form of government—except for all the others that have been tried…" A funny quote given the context; merely months after the end of World War Two, he was voted out of office.

The thing about democracy is that it is cumbersome, and it is, by its very nature, laden with administrative bureaucratic challenges. Despite that, it is the only way to ensure that the nation moves according to the general will of the populace.

As the renowned Republican political philosopher, Jean Jacques Rousseau, put it, "The General Will is always right."

The only way to discover the general will is through voting.

Only through action can you influence the general will of the nation. The general will requires a majority, which means—assuming that the statistics are correct and that approximately two-thirds of the voting population voted in the last election—we need to influence 79 million people.

Sitting in your basement telling horror stories is not enacting change. If you have the time to tell scary stories around the digital campfire, then you certainly have the time to get off the couch and get involved.

Governance is the essence, and the county is the beginning of our entire governance system.

People said, "We're not happy with Pence; we think Pence choked!" The real problem is that, by the time a sufficient challenge could be raised in 2020, the result had already been through the states and Congress. The errors occurred at the very beginning, at the polls in the counties; that is the fault of the citizens in failing to hold their counties accountable. If we work together, we will not allow this to happen again.

Chapter Twelve

The Portrait of a Great America

"For those who've abandoned hope, we'll restore hope and we'll welcome them into a great national crusade to make America great again."

Ronald Reagan

Democracy is a wonderful thing. It allows every citizen to have a say and moves with consensus. This means that every political opinion is valid. This fight is a fight that we have to fight together, accepting that we have differing political opinions.

This is not a book that is aimed solely at Republicans. Far from it. This enemy does not only exist within the Democrats, but it also exists within the GOP. If it only existed on the Blue side of the aisle, then Bush W. would never have instigated the Forever War action off the back of 9/11. We would have dealt with it quickly, decisively.

And that is not to say that all Democrats are Deep Staters. It is, though, where the Deep State has found the most success because in the name of "progressive politics," they can encourage the abandonment of God and promote degeneration.

As a result, we NEED Democrats to fight with us. We need you guys to challenge the corruption within your party, just as Republicans challenge the corruption in theirs. If Democrats do not join us, then the Deep State gets what it wants. It gets division, which inhibits unity and purpose.

In a Great America, we remove the layers of red tape that the bureaucracy hides behind. We live under God, accepting His word as truth and live according to His values. We live by healthy boundaries and American values, accepting that everyone has a right to vote and to express their opinion.

In a Great America, we stand up for liberty; we defend freedom. We recognize that we may not always agree with one another's opinions, but we will die to defend the right to express them.

But what does a Great America look like? In the battle for control, and to defend our liberty and our nation, how do we know we have won? What does a Great America look like?

Citizens Are Actively Leading Their Counties

A Great America is an America in which democracy has truly manifested. It is an America where citizens are actively leading their counties. Sure, we have representatives, but those representatives work at our behest. These elected and appointed leaders act very, very differently when they know they are being watched and held accountable.

How do they know what we want?

They know what we want because we are heard. We are politically and socially active, and we make our voices heard. We move according to consensus, accepting that we all have differing opinions but are united in our common American identity, guided by our determination to see our nation succeed.

In a Great America, we are united under God. Under His guidance, we protect liberty and freedom, and we lead the global charge against authoritarianism, globalism, and tyranny once again.

It is our right to expect our nation to work for us, but we also have to work for our nation. In a Great America, we protect one another despite the differences between us, and we do it because we are all American, and we all stand for the same set of values, even if we disagree on the ways in which we get there.

That is what politics is for. That is why we vote. In a Great America, we reject the division bestowed upon us by the Deep State, and we unite ourselves through our love of God, our country, and our way of life. We do not automatically reject someone based on their political opinion. We engage in healthy debate, making genuine attempts to see things from the points of view of others.

This unity, these healthy relationships that we will have forged, make it possible for us, as Americans, to lead the way on the global stage and to provide security to those who promote freedom and democracy all over the world. We wake the world up from its doleful reverence of the notion of global governance, showing them the dangers of the WEF, the UN, and supranational agencies whose goal is to govern.

I believe that there is a place for security pacts—for pacts that enable nations to defend one another and protect those who are vulnerable—but not the way that these pacts have been leveraged to form supranational governments. This is the basis on which the EU was formed, and Great Britain rightly saw sense and walked away from that madness.

In a Great America, law enforcement and intelligence work together, but for the benefit of the citizens not against them. Liberty means the right to live with our human rights intact but with the protection given to us that our taxes pay for.

In a Great America, entrepreneurial spirit thrives, and technologies are developed for societal benefit. At present, we live in a world where technology is developed to further the control that these tech giants already have over our lives and they sign over to governments, both domestic and internationally. And believe me, your secrets are available to governments all over the world. Anyone who uses TikTok, a company which is owned by the Chinese government, has already sold their soul to the Chinese Communist Party devil. A Great America protects Americans from such ridiculousness, from such danger.

I joined this battle for one reason, to serve the people of America once more. I have devoted my life to serving the people of the United States of America, and I would gladly do it all over again. It is here, in this battle, that I know I can and will have the greatest impact on American liberty. It is in this arena, and on this battlefield, that I can put my skills to the greatest use.

I, and many others, have crafted and perfected this image of a Great America. And love him or hate him, the image that President Trump gave to us with his red hats and the MAGA brand was one that provided and allowed for each of these great tenets. I believe wholeheartedly in Trump's Make America Great Again mantra because it ascribes to each of the aspects of American civilization that I referenced before. It laid bare the lies and the idiosyncrasies that previous administrations have allowed to infect the core of our politics and our very way of life.

Secure Your County and the Nation Will Follow

To achieve this vision of a Great America, you have to get off the couch in your county. Only you and your fellow citizens can deliver a Great America.

Matt Weinglass is a producer, director, and storyteller who has made a living telling the authentic stories of people challenging power in Latin America. Matt is a man who sits on the left of the political spectrum, but recognizes, like me and anyone else reading this book, that we need to work together to overthrow the Deep State and the globalist actors it serves.

He has been politically active for years. In 2000, he went door-to-door on the campaign trail to encourage people to vote Democrat and redefine Centrism.

But Matt also knows that, in the fight for control, ideology does not matter. Sure, we all have our values, but he recognizes that those values should come from a place that serves the nation and the society it protects.

To highlight this to me, he presented me with his Kite Model. Take a look.

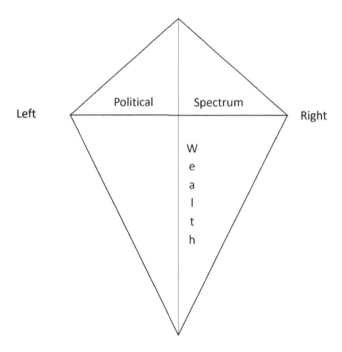

This model highlights how we take back control, and how it relies on uniting those from both sides of the aisle and engaging those below the peak of the Kite to fight back.

Allow me to elaborate. At the top of this Kite, you have the supreme clerics of the Deep State. These are the plutocrats, the globalists. Beneath them, fanning out to the left and right of the political spectrum, you have the bureaucrats and the technocrats, those who serve their whims and promote their interests within Congress, the Pentagon, and the White House. They have no political allegiance; they simply back the horse that offers them the best avenue to power and control.

At the bottom of the Kite, you have the lowest earners, those who live in poverty or adversity. Often, they do not have the luxury of political activism because, for them, life is a daily grind that requires all of their attention.

As you climb the wealth ladder, the percentage of the population grows, as does the variety of political allegiance and opinion. In our current system, one which is fueled and fed by the Deep State, this represents a divide. This divide weakens us, presenting a diasporic effect on the strength that we present as a nation.

The goal, then, is to unite the left and the right on one common goal: using the strength we have in our numbers to surge up the Kite and uppercut the elites.

We achieve this through political activism, through standing up to the enemy and empowering and uplifting those around us. As we do, we motivate those in our communities, and we create a surge of energy and power that the Deep State cannot resist. We unify around our common goal, and our political differences serve to strengthen us instead of weaken us, providing the diversity needed to envisage a range of responses and actions.

Matt shares my belief that if we are opposed to one another, caught in a civil form of gang warfare, then we will not unite. Not in a system that has been designed to promote class warfare where we are baited to hate one another in a vicious cycle that cracks our foundations and takes away our stability, our power, and opens us up to vulnerability.

Only together can we fight them, and the Kite shows this. If we allow the political divide to weaken us, then we give them what they want. Through direct action, we provide the tools to those less fortunate, uplifting and strengthening them by helping to draft new policies and overthrowing the policies that have deliberately been enacted to create division throughout society.

Matt, being a storyteller, highlights the need to speak their language, to use the tools that they have mastered as the ultimate weapon against them. Here, he is referring to the media. The Deep State–controlled media are masters of propaganda, so we have to get the language right as storytellers. We have to put our words out on the page and the screen.

Most importantly, we have to do it in a way that is universally attractive and recognizable. Yes, there are many in this fight using these tactics already, but they limit themselves by using language that appeals to highly limited demographics, often in the image of the creator. We get this right, and we pull in the masses, moving with a unified purpose as, one-by-one, eyes open and purposes are actualized.

Sure, on the surface this may sound like the utopia that the Deep State is striving for: everyone acting in one mind, moving in one direction, serving one purpose. I can assure you, though, this definitely is not that. It is far from that. It is one in which political differences and viewpoints are celebrated and recognized for what they are: attempts to move the nation in a direction that serves America.

A direction that serves Americans. A direction that serves God.

A Constitutional, America First Model Starting with the County

Our Constitution is the gift our Founding Fathers gave to us. In a liberated Great America, we hold our Constitution almost as close to our hearts as we do the Holy Bible. This is the sword and the shield that we will use to cut down the enemy.

Even Jesus came with a figurative sword. Jesus was prepared to fight, and to die.

I have already spoken of the virtues of an America First model. In a Great America, we will thrive and grow under a Constitutional, America

First model. The Constitution was designed to promote and protect the freedoms and liberties of American citizens, and it is that, and the grace of God, that I believe has made this the greatest nation on Earth.

If we live by the tenets of an America First model, we protect our borders. We recognize that it is not racist to want to have a proactive discussion about border control. Yes, we may not all agree on the way in which we do it, but what we shall agree on is that it needs to be done. Our citizens deserve that protection; they deserve not to have opportunity stolen from them by caravans of people overwhelming our defenses and degrading our sovereignty.

If we live by the tenets of an America First model, we reject globalism, undermining and challenging the international strength of the global Deep State. Our nation is overwhelmingly powerful on the international stage. If we remove the indecision and the weakness that has stagnated our influence, then we can once again exert our influence on the globe and defend the world from the biological terrorism of China and Russian imperialism.

We can promote the word of God and His virtue, uniting the world in the fight against oppression. Our America First model will serve as the inspiration as each nation adopts its own Nation First models. This is how we strengthen ourselves. This is how the world brings itself to equilibrium, creating firm borders and rejecting their own individual cadres of Deep State elites and actors. When the world recognizes the evil, the world will pull together to fight it.

Angela Beckles is a wonderful woman with whom I share a church. She is the most politically active member of the congregation, serving, in her own words, as "the unofficial political liaison," and a former special policy advisor. Angela believes, like me, that more Christians should be actively involved in politics in their state and their county. As a result, for the last ten years she has been inviting elected officials or people who have been running for office, including figures like former Virginia Governor George Allen and Glenn Youngkin.

As a result of her activism, she was actively reached out to by the Trump campaign. She speaks with great pride about being reached out to directly by President Trump's people based in Trump Tower in New York. As a result, she holds amazing influence among her peers and is a shining example of what we are looking to achieve. She is gathering support and political motivation, and she is doing so to help reinstate civilian control in the county. In her own words:

"The people in this country's real political power is with the political bodies closest to them…the state, the county…people that we have elected to those offices. We are able to address and have dialogue with our local government and have a bigger effect on our daily lives, whereas with the federal government, where do you go for grievances?"

She speaks, based on her own experiences, of how red tape and bureaucracy makes it impossible to influence national politics, and how the bureaucrats protect that system, making it immensely difficult to pass effective legislation because they know that every four to eight years, the elected officials around them will be gone. In her words, "the bureaucrats run the country." Only at the local level can we challenge this.

By protecting our rights as enshrined in the Constitution, and by recognizing them as the guidelines that promote American self-interest and protection, we return power to the people to whom it was originally bequeathed. We fight against the enemy that threatens to engulf us and enslave us.

The frontline troops in this battle to regain control do not wear camouflaged uniforms and helmets, they dress smart casual. They do not fly fighter jets and drive tanks to war. They drive sedans to soccer practice.

They are you.

The only way to retake control, to return America to the power of its citizens, is to get off the couch, to protect the integrity of our elections, and to fight the lunacy of centralized, global governance.

It is to flip the bird at Klaus Schwab, at Silicon Valley, at the UN, and the WEF and its crony organizations by pulling the rug from under the feet at the most local of levels.

The first weapon of this Citizen Army is the ballot. We must protect the ballot at all costs. We have to allow the voice of the people to be heard in its truest form. We cannot allow the Deep State to manipulate our system to serve their needs. Not anymore.

The second weapon is the word of God. "For we do not wrestle against flesh and blood, but against the rulers, against the authorities, against the cosmic powers over this present darkness, against the spiritual forces of evil in the heavenly places."[16]

God is with us in the fight, and by fighting alongside Him, we protect the Christian values that gave us the strength to create this great nation. We overthrow indecency; we reject immorality. "Put to death therefore what is earthly in you: sexual immorality, impurity, passion, evil desire, and covetousness, which is idolatry."[17]

By living according to the Bible (and yes, again, we are a diverse country of different faiths to communicate inclusiveness), establishing solid boundaries, and celebrating righteous lifestyles, we remember what it is to be American. We Make America Great Again.

The battlefield is YOUR county. Do not concern yourself with other counties. Fight for YOUR county, and the nation will follow.

Just like the amazing moms of Loudoun County, steel yourself. Do not allow yourself to be fooled into thinking that consuming the material of QAnon and other freedom fighters is a form of action.

---

16. Ephesians 6:12.
17. Colossians 3:5.

The only action is that which gets you off the couch, in front of school boards, in council meetings. It is in securing the integrity of our elections. It is motivating those around you and uniting them. It is being seen, being heard, not shrinking into silence. Find your strength in the example set by these warriors.

In this war, you are the soldier.

In this war, you are the hero.

Congratulations!

All "The Nation Will Follow" readers can pre-order a copy today of "Moms Will Win This War: A Roll Call for Revolutionary Pastors, Parents, and Patriots"

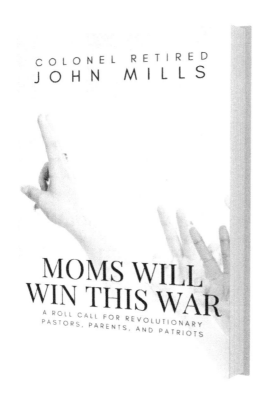

www.TheNationWillFollow.com

BONUS

Exclusive Interview with Jovan Pulitzer on the moment that Colonel Ret. John discovered the Deep State's dark agenda in the White House.

Available Now at www.TheNationWillFollow.com

Pierucci Publishing

Elevating World Consciousness Through Books

www.PierucciPublishing.com

If you're a devoted pastor, patriot, or parent, we're looking for your story.

Email Publishing@PierucciPublishing.com

Join The Patriot Revolution

What would it mean to live in a world where Parents, Pastors, and Patriots like me and you have our voices heard and our votes counted? What would that world look like for your children and grandchildren? Help us construct a new, fair, empowered system in place of the crumbling Deep State tyranny.

Here's how you share the Patriot Revolution with your community.

1. **Download Your Bonus Program** right now at www. TheNationWillFollow.com

2. **Give this book to empowered Patriots.** Email blueshadowucq@ verizon.net if you'd like to purchase bulk copies for family, friends, and local political or school board officials.

3. **Give this book to your library.** Your library isn't going to seek out this "controversial" blueprint to a Patriot revolution, so supply it for them. Perhaps your town has free libraries in strategic locations; supply those free libraries with *The Nation Will Follow* so that we can get the message out to our community.

4. **Ask** Barnes and Noble or other Bookstores to order *The Nation Will Follow.* Once enough people demand *The Nation Will Follow,* bookstores will begin carrying the book and giving it increasingly more desirable shelf space.

5. **Write an amazing five-star review** wherever you purchased this book and/or wherever you love buying books.

6. **Follow Colonel Ret John on all social platforms.**

   On Gettr: ColonelRETJohn

   On Truth: ColonelRETJohn

   Regularly on:

   > Epoch Times at https://www.theepochtimes.com/author-john-mills

   > NewsMax at https://www.newsmax.com/

   > …and Center for Security Policy

   > https://centerforsecuritypolicy.org/author/john-mills/

In Freedom,

Colonel Ret John

Made in the USA
Monee, IL
18 March 2023

30158584R10103